The Spiritual Woman

The Spiritual Woman

TRUSTEE OF THE FUTURE

"The eternal woman leads us upward."
—GOETHE

EDITED BY

MARION TURNER SHEEHAN

Harper & Brothers Publishers

New York

THE SPIRITUAL WOMAN

Library of Congress catalog card number: 55-6971

CONTRIBUTORS

FRANCES P. BOLTON, Congresswoman, House of Representatives, Twenty-second District, Ohio. Member, Foreign Affairs Committee. Sponsor of Bolton Act for creation of U.S. Cadet Nurse Corps. Sponsor of Bill for Low-Rent Public Housing Units. Trustee, Tuskegee Institute, Alabama; Lake Erie College, Painesville, Ohio; Meharry Medical College, Nashville, Tennessee. Vice-President, American Social Hygiene Association.

ESTHER EBERSTADT BROOKE, Author, Lecturer, Management Consultant on personnel problems to international business and industrial leaders. Founding Member, The Junior League of the Oranges, N. J. Life Member, The Assistance League of Southern California; The Metropolitan Museum of Art; The American Museum of Natural History; The American National Theatre and Academy. Life Fellow, The American Geographical Society. Member, The Capitol Hill Club, Washington, D. C.; The Author's Guild. Member, Board of Directors, Philharmonic Society of New York. Author of *Career Guide; Guide to Career Success; You and Your Personality.*

PATRICIA CROWLEY, Housewife. Co-founder of the Christian Family Movement, Chicago, Illinois. Co-sponsor of *Act,* CFM bimonthly newsletter.

LILLIAN GISH, Actress, Lecturer, Philanthropist. Member, Actor's Equity.

VALERIE HARVEY, R.N. Chief Therapist, Kenny Institute, Jersey City Medical Center, New Jersey.

JANE M. HOEY, Director of Social Research, National Tuberculosis Association, New York City. Director, Federal Bureau of Public Assistance, Social Security Administration, Washington, D.C. 1936–54. Assistant Director and Secretary of the Health Division, Welfare Council of New York City, 1926–36. Trustee, New York School of

v

Contributors

Social Work. Secretary of the U.S. Committee of International Conference of Social Work. Alternate Representative of U.S. to Sixth, Seventh, and Eighth Sessions of the Social Commission of the Economic and Social Council of the United Nations.

ALICE V. KELIHER, Professor, Department of Early Childhood and Elementary Education, New York University School of Education. Associate Professor, Yale University Clinic for Child Development. Sponsor of Citizens Committee on Children, New York City, Member, U.S. Attorney-General's Conference on Juvenile Delinquency. Chairman, War and Mobilization, Mid-Century White House Conference, 1950. Author of *Life and Growth; A Critical Study of Homogeneous Grouping.*

SISTER ELIZABETH KENNY, Founder, Sister Elizabeth Kenny Foundation, Kenny Institute, Minneapolis, Minnesota; The Eastern Area Kenny Institute, Jersey City Medical Center; the Kenny Clinic, Buffalo; the Kenny Institute, Pontiac, Michigan; the Kenny Institute, El Monte, California.

ILONA MASSEY, Actress, Lecturer. Member, Actor's Equity; American Federation of Television and Radio Artists; American Guild Variety Artists.

ANNE O'HARE McCORMICK, Foreign Correspondent, News Analyst, Columnist, Journalist, Author. U.S. Delegate to UNESCO 1946–48. Member, National Institute Arts and Letters. Vice-President, New York Newspaper Women's Club; Overseas Press Club. Chevalier of National Order of the Legion of Honor. Winner of Pulitzer Prize; Woman's National Press Club Achievement Award, 1945; Medal for Eminent Achievement of the American Woman's Association, 1939.

MILLICENT C. McINTOSH, President, Barnard College, New York City. Trustee, Bryn Mawr College, Bryn Mawr, Pennsylvania. President, Guild of Independent Schools, New York City. Director, Home Life Insurance Company of New York. Trustee, American Museum of Natural History. Member, Advisory Committee, John Hay Whitney Foundation.

MARY T. NORTON, Congresswoman, House of Representatives, Thirteenth District, New Jersey, 1924–54. Sponsor of Wage and Hour Law, Fair Employment Practices Committee. Advisor to International Labor Conference, Paris, 1945. Consultant to the U.S. Secretary of Labor on Womanpower, Washington, D.C.

Contributors

ELIZABETH S. RIDDER, Housewife. Co-founder, Casita Maria Community Center, New York. Volunteer Member, National Board of Girl Scouts, and Member of National Executive Committee. National Secretary of the Girl Scouts of the United States of America.

MARION TURNER SHEEHAN, Editor, Lecturer. Co-author of *Citizenship Training Program in the Schools*. Co-associate to the editor of *The Netherlands*, University of California Press. First Vice-President, American Woman's Association. Member, Board of Directors, New York League of Business and Professional Women. Member, St. Paul's Guild, New York; Oriel Society, New York. Founder-President, Woman's World Council for Moral Values, Inc., New York.

ELOISE SPAETH, Trustee, Dayton Ohio Art Institute. American Representative, Venetian Biennale, Venice, Italy, 1952. Trustee, Vice-President, American Federation of Arts, and Chairman of Exhibition Service.

HELEN C. WHITE, Professor of Literature, University of Wisconsin. Member, U.S. National Commission for UNESCO, 1946–49; Education Mission to Germany, 1946; Board of Directors of National Conference of Christians and Jews; Council of Modern Language Association, 1944–1947. President, American Association University Women, 1941–1947. Vice-President, International Federation University Women. Author of *The Metaphysical Poets; The Tudor Books of Private Devotion; Seventeenth-Century Verse and Prose*.

CONTENTS

Contents

From women's eyes this doctrine I derive;
They sparkle still the right Promethean fire;
They are the books, the arts, the academies,
That show, contain and nourish
All the world.

—WILLIAM SHAKESPEARE

FOREWORD

Anne O'Hare McCormick

Just after the devouring and devastating machine of war had smashed its way across Europe, I made a reporter's journey through the wreckage. It took me from one end of the vast battle-field to the other, from the craters of London to the rubble of Budapest, from the shattered port of Le Havre to the Pompeii-like desolation of Naples. I saw terrible sights—and inspiring sights. Today the material reconstruction is so spectacular that it is difficult to recall the extent of the ruin, but in the wake of the Allied armies—armies that had to destroy in order to liberate—there were already signs of what I can only describe as life ever-lasting: the invincible determination of human beings to rise out of the deadly dust and start over again.

The signs were little things, the gestures of little people, yet it seemed to me then, and in spite of the disappointed hopes of the years between it seems to me now, that those individual gestures were bigger with promise for the future than great political events. Cities were prostrate, communication was paralyzed, but the spirit of ordinary men and women was alive.

One of these little things, recorded in a dispatch from France in March 1945, the Editor is kind enough to say was the seed of this book. "The Woman with a Broom" inspired her to ask a number of wise women, each distinguished in her special field, to contribute to a symposium on the place of woman in the postwar world. The general theme is that women, and particularly American women in a time when the United States is thrust into a position of unique power and influence, have the soul of the nation in their keeping. They have a special obligation to emphasize, preserve, and manifest in their own lives the spiritual values that are in danger of being lost in an age in which skepticism is a virtue and faith a vice.

The purpose of this book is to stir the consciences of American women, regardless of race or color, creed or class, to make a fight to save the moral standards and the belief in God which the Founding Fathers wrote into the Constitution. Before woman can play her proper part in the struggle of our time, she has to take a fresh look at herself and decide in what fields her contribution to society can make the strongest and most lasting impact upon the community. Her first responsibility is to know herself and to have a philosophy of life to guide her inner thoughts and her outer actions.

Here is the little piece that sparked the enterprise. I am honored to have it reproduced as a preface to a summons to women, from women leaders, to be worthy of their spiritual heritage and deeply aware that they share the work of creation and mold the future. "When God erases," said Bossuet, "He is beginning to write." When women clear away the debris of war, instinctively they are trying to restore God's order in the chaos man has made.

THE WOMAN WITH A BROOM [1]

"Every correspondent who has been near the front has seen the woman with the broom described by John MacCormac in a dispatch from the United States Ninth Army Headquarters east of the Rhine. In a devastated town two miles behind the fighting line he observed a woman emerge from a cellar and, though her house was a ruin, proceed to sweep away the dust and rubble that covered the doorstep.

"This woman happened to be German, but in every war-ravaged country the woman with a broom trying to clear away the debris that used to be her home is as familiar and monotonous a

[1] Excerpts from "Bulldozer and the Woman with a Broom" by Anne O'Hare McCormick, *The New York Times,* March 28, 1945.

sight as ruin itself. In one flattened village in Holland after another, dazed old men were standing in wavering clusters in the
shell-pocked fields, but the women were working in the door-
yards that a few hours before had led to houses. Several were
trying to tie their chrysanthemum stalks to the poles that had
held them up. The chrysanthemums were still blooming, bright
yellow beside piles of brick dust, and the housewives were
mechanically starting to save the one whole thing that survived
the wreck of the shattered cottages. . . .

"But the woman in Evreux, in battered Normandy, was not
thinking so far ahead when she appeared with her broom that
bleak Sunday morning and began raising the dust in the path of
General de Gaulle and the distinguished visitors from Paris. With
a dash and energy as impatient as General Patton's, as he sweeps
across the German plain, she was making a broomstick attack
upon the crumbled stones that lay atop a tiny patch of garden.
She paid no attention to the cortege skirting the shell holes in the
road until a woman in the party stopped to ask her what she
thought she was doing with a broom in the wake of 2,000-pound
bombs. 'Who's to save the cabbages and onions if I don't?' They're
all that's left of all the work of all my life,' she said fiercely. 'And
somebody has to begin clearing away this mess.'

"Then there was the old woman sweeping out a cowshed in the
Agro Romano, near Rome. The land had been flooded by the
Germans and was once more a breeding place for malarial mos-
quitoes, banished by the efforts of fifty years. The house was gone.
In a fifty-mile radius not an animal was left. The farmer, who had
lost a hand in a minefield, looked at us with hopeless eyes; but the
woman kept on sweeping, clearing a little space in the wreckage
to begin life anew.

"The woman with a broom is both symbol and promise. It's
pretty futile to start attacking the ruins of great cities with a
kitchen broom. Yet everywhere before the monster bulldozers
arrive to clear paths for the armies through the debris left by
the bombers, women instinctively seize their brooms in this age-
old gesture of cleaning up the mess the men have made.

Foreword

"There's no assurance that they can clear it up this time, but today there are more women than men in Europe, widows of soldiers, widows of hostages, widows of the last war, and they are bound to try. In Paris an association of widows of men executed by the Germans is headed by a lovely girl widow. . . . 'We are the trustees of the future,' the French girl asserted. 'We cannot leave it to the next generation because they won't have seen what we have seen, and they won't understand.

"It isn't chance that women are named for the first time to a conference called to set up the framework of international order. There should be more of them, for they are in the wars now, and millions of them have nothing much left but a broom. . . ."

PREFACE

America, with *seven* per cent of the world's population, has *forty* per cent of the total world income. This material advantage, accumulated through the years, is substantial and provides a favored position of influence. We are able to underwrite the economies of stricken nations; we can help the growth of political forms to supplant the crumbled structures of the past. But are these the only things that cry out for reconstruction? What of the need to restore the spiritual value of human life trampled upon by dictators and distorted by false philosophers? It is with this kind of restoration that woman, as trustee, must primarily concern herself for the sake of future generations.

Because there is a moral crisis in the world, there is a need for militant faith in God on the part of every conscientious woman. Today's woman must be actively dedicated to God to triumph over anti-God forces and to secure our spiritual survival. Women of religious conviction will see that moral maturity must be kept abreast of material growth if lasting peace in the world is to prevail. There is something of God in every person and a lack of reference to the Divine can deprive humanity of its spiritual and cultural heritage and, therefore, of its freedom.

The new world of today and tomorrow must not be a "woman's world" any more than the old world should have been a "man's world." The *domination* of either sex over the other is a violation of the order of God. The leadership of human society is man's assignment from the Creator. And for a successful leadership there is need for both sexes to contribute harmoniously their special aptitudes and gifts. The ideal is not displacement or isolation, or provocative competition, but, rather, association, reciprocal, compatible exchange through the cooperative exercise of the endowments of both man and woman.

The spiritual nourishment of the race is the special mission of the eternal woman whose unique position has inspired mankind for centuries. The change in the civil rights of woman over the past century has pinpointed the need to rethink her functions and influence in modern society. After the fury and emotion of extremism, we are ready to apply ourselves more thoughtfully and calmly to contributing to society, for its spiritual and cultural enrichment, those qualities which are distinctly feminine.

Today's clash of competitive personalities between man and woman must be transformed into a collaboration of complementary gifts for the benefit of society. We need to restore and protect spiritual and moral values in every phase of our living. Women who believe in God must bring about the restoration of His Law and Order because the attempt to discredit the authority of God over human life is gaining strength in many lands. By not recognizing the strength of this threat, people sensitive to spiritual values may allow the spiritually insensitive to gain control in many areas of influence. They may try to lull us with the assurance that in spite of America's overemphasis on materialism and the growing disregard of moral standards, Americans in the face of direct challenge will somehow rise with the spiritual vitality needed to sustain our liberties, our homes and our country. But such assurance cannot be realistically accepted. History has proved that in countries where spiritual and cultural values were all but buried, there were not the faith, hope and fortitude present to face the issue squarely and defeat the enemy. We can maintain peace *only* if responsible men and women take action *now* to strengthen the spiritual and moral forces we must depend upon if we wish to survive in a free world.

Woman should be interested naturally in the offspring that will come forth from the travail of society in the twentieth century. It should bear her features as well as the features of man, thus only can it be truly representative of humanity. The conscientious woman's desire today is to participate according to her feminine capacity in the formation of a new world which will demand deeper spiritual foundation than this society that is passing. She will make a lasting contribution when she realizes her responsibility to impress upon society at this time the supreme importance of a spiritual vision.

All the contributors to this symposium have analyzed their various fields of feminine endeavor and influence with complete freedom to express their own ideas. They do not compel agreement nor do they take responsibility for other than their own chapters. Naturally, the reader would not be expected to agree completely with the many points of view expressed. But it is noteworthy that all these women are agreed upon the need of a total effort for the restoration of spiritual and moral values in all areas of life. As a part of their contribution to this need, editor and contributors have arranged with the publisher to donate this book's royalties to organizations whose members are active in furthering this restoration both here and abroad.

MARION TURNER SHEEHAN

New York City, N.Y.

The Spiritual Woman

I

ELOISE SPAETH

Woman in the Arts

WHAT does woman, as woman, contribute to the arts? What is her place in music, painting, sculpture, letters? What is her sphere of influence? Does she have the power, the capacity, the dedication to create and bring to fruition a work of art? Or is she best suited to interpreting the work of another? Is she more properly, for instance, the musician, who is, in effect, another instrument for the composer? Or is her true home in the arts in that narrow border region where an actress, while interpreting the work of the playwright, is all the same creating herself a character, a mood?

In an age in which the equality of the sexes in most countries is underwritten by constitutional guarantees, we women like to think that we can stand beside our brothers in the creative world. Yet who can name one great woman composer? Down the chords of time, from Palestrina to Bach, Beethoven, Brahms, to Sibelius, Stravinsky, Hindemith, Copeland, where are the feminine grace notes? The Renaissance dazzled itself and succeeding ages with its largesse of great painters: Botticelli, Fra Angelico, Leonardo, Michelangelo, Raphael. Was there a woman? None has survived. In seventeenth- and eighteenth-century Venice it would seem that every other man held a painter's brush or a sculptor's

1

tool; only one woman's name comes down to us: Rosalba Carriera. Famous throughout Italy for her portraits, she swept through France to remember for us the look of the famous and beautiful, La Pompadour, Louis XV. She introduced pastel, the soft-colored crayon, to French painting. Her final accolade as a painter came when Watteau, at the height of his own powers, when every woman in France dressed and moved according to his work, asked her to paint his portrait. At about the same time the Dutch school gave us Rachel Ruysch, a painter of still life, whose reputation is second only to Jan van Huysum's. Once again, however, in a time and place burgeoning with artists, hers is the only feminine talent to be found. And when the great Dutch Exhibition was held in London in 1929, with paintings brought from all over the world, no woman was included. By comparison with the masters, the women were minor painters.

In eighteenth-century France, a rich period containing artists like Fragonard, Watteau, Boucher, one woman stands out, Vigée Lebrun. The protégée of Marie Antoinette, Lebrun did more than a dozen portraits of that gay, unfortunate queen. The clang of the guillotine that fell on Marie Antoinette's stem-like neck sent Vigée Lebrun hurrying into exile across the Channel. In England she traveled through the country and painted every aspect of the rural green. Lebrun is also remembered for her portrait of another great and unhappy beauty, Lady Hamilton. Rosa Bonheur, whose long life almost reached our own century, was certainly the greatest woman painter of animals. Her famous picture, "Horse Fair," rejected by her native Bordeaux at a price of 15,000 francs, finally fetched 268,000 francs from Cornelius Vanderbilt, who gave it in 1887 to the Metropolitan Museum. Her long, prolific career was crowned by receiving, though surreptitiously, the Cross of the Legion of Honor. The gallant gentlemen of France guarded greedily this coveted honor. Sentiment was so against its going to a woman, no matter what her achievement, that it had to be given to Bonheur by the Empress Eugénie acting as Regent while the Emperor was out of town.

2

In the Impressionist and Post-Impressionist periods, so recently past, women fared better: Berthe Morisot and Mary Cassatt, while not innovators in that age of innovations, showed talents that entitle them to hang with the masters, Renoir, Cézanne, Pissarro, Monet, Seurat, Van Gogh, Degas. At present, probably more women are painting seriously than ever before, but while many of them are turning out canvases of sensitivity and distinction, none has yet been bracketed with Picasso or Matisse. But that woman can create in paint the symbols, protests, miseries of social upheaval, is powerfully shown in the work of the German Käthe Kollwitz.

Heartening as is the work of this handful of artists, past and present, the women are all of them exceptional, lonely, against the grain. Historically and currently alike, it is in writing that woman's creative forces blossom, and given a maturing summer, bear fruit more frequently. Perhaps this is due to the light from Sappho's torch, reflected and kept burning down the ages.

At any rate, in the tenth century we find a Benedictine nun, Hroswitha, court poetess and playwright to Otto I of Germany. In her work are the literary origins of Faust and Romeo and Juliet, and a wealth of material that astonished her nineteenth-century translators. Héloïse's letters to Abélard record forever the soul of a woman in love and do so on the same level of discourse as her lover, the most brilliant philosopher of his day. Today the prose of St. Theresa of Avila throbs with the same power it had when she wrote three hundred years ago. St. Catherine of Siena, whose work fills eleven volumes, ranks close to Petrarch in Italian literature. Christine de Pisane in her poetry set the moral and courtly tone for two French regimes, those of Charles V and Charles VI. Jane Austen, sunk in what was supposed to be the stultifying atmosphere of the provinces, created a gallery of the most penetrating character studies in literature. From the dreary moor of Yorkshire the Brontës gave us two powerfully imaginative novels, *Jane Eyre* and *Wuthering Heights*. In our own day, Virginia Woolf, Rebecca West, Elinor Wylie, Edith Wharton,

3

Carson McCullers, Eudora Welty, Elizabeth Bowen, Sigrid Undset, Edna St. Vincent Millay are but a few of the writers accepted by critics and readers with pleasure. Yet, in spite of woman's relatively brilliant showing in literature, each name mentioned is, in its own time and in historical perspective, overshadowed by a greater name and a man's. Our women writers have done beautiful, moving work; they have never been the masters of an age, nor are they now.

All this is said, all these lists are drawn up and comparisons made not to begin a battle of the sexes, but to demonstrate one overwhelming fact about woman in art. There is no point in showing that in some fields woman comes off second-best, in others she simply isn't there. Nor is the intent to deny woman's creative capacity. This summing up does not mean inequality. It simply means that woman's role in the arts is different from man's. A mallet and a chisel are equally important in carving a statue, but they do not have the same functions. It is the same with man and woman. Of every great artist we can ask, confident of the answer, "What woman made this possible? Who was the inspiration, who the critic whose gentle objectivity guided him? Who was his shield against wastrel distractions, whose the insistent voice that constantly restored a frequently faltering confidence?" Whether wife or mother, mistress, sweetheart, sister, you find her—perhaps not even acknowledged—but there.

This essential relationship was clouded over when the feminists demanded equal rights for women. Social, economic, and legal equality are so necessary to woman's dignity, so rightfully a part of her being, that discussion is absurd. Unhappily, enthusiasm for that just cause made the false assumption that woman is as competent as man in any field. The assumption is exploded by reversing it; if A is equal to B, then B must be equal to A, but no one pretends that man is as able as woman to operate the home, that most complex and surprising and difficult of human milieux. Yet that false assumption has turned many a good mother into a bad artist, has so warped her sense of values that

4

she sometimes thinks more of turning out a second-rate painting than of bringing up a first-rate child.

In procreation lies woman's power and glory. Her responsibility begins with the first stirring in her womb. With the child's dawning awareness, woman begins her work of molding, instilling, exciting a love for beauty. While he is still a child, woman leads man to an understanding of art, to the integrity and power that go into its creation. She shows him that beauty is not only pleasing to the eye, but that through the eye it reaches every corner of the human soul. We may well ask ourselves where we have failed in this sacred trust. Would so many of our churches be filled with the horrors they contain, the painted monstrosities called statues which distract instead of embellish, which sicken instead of elevate, if the mothers of our priests and ministers had made the art gallery, the museum, the concert hall as intimately part of their children's early training as the movies, the radio, the comics? Raising a family is a time-consuming, energy-consuming business, but the mother who makes time for art is both doing her duty to her children and creating little islands of peace where mother and children can grow together in love for beauty. In art, money is no object. The poorest mother is not without means at her command as a citizen; the free library and museum, the record library, are now almost universal. By using these and other opportunities that present themselves, she can make her children rich indeed.

Geniuses in art, as elsewhere, are made for or lost to the world by women. The mother's role is a most important one. The genius who is not given a sense of values early, who is not taught self-discipline, rarely utilizes his gift to the full. His mother must nurture and channel his talent, guard it from exploitation until the boy himself is ready to take command of his angel. Twenty-five years ago, there were *two* violin prodigies who arrived together at the age of twelve. Menuhin alone survives. He was shielded from a fawning public, marched home after every concert, encouraged in small-boy play but given the sense that

5

his gift was almost a public trust. Ignoring a fully booked season his mother abruptly withdrew him from performance during the difficult adolescent years, to mature and work in quiet. The other boy, a genuinely gifted youngster, was exploited to the full, played concert after concert, forced to practice for hours, then indulged, lionized, spoiled. At eighteen, when Menuhin reappeared to begin a distinguished career that has delighted the world ever since, the second boy was at his end, a victim of his mother's avarice, lightheadedness and lack of understanding of her own role.

Woman as the artist's wife is no less important. With body and spirit she gives him a place to stand, from which he may measure the whole universe. She can subtly control the intensity of his inner flame, preserving him from the ravages of too great immersion in art, encouraging him when despondency or inertia comes, as they must. She rears the children so that he is free to work; she learns juggling with money so that it gives him no worry; she crushes her own desires for play and material comforts. Such a woman makes a great contribution to art; frequently she spells the difference between achievement and frustration in her artist husband. We all know cases where a fine talent has been wasted because the artist's creative energy has been dissipated to meet the demands of an extravagant, party-girl wife.

Woman does not become guardian of man's creativity by wishing. She must prepare herself for beauty. In the time allowed her, she must study, read, observe, seize every opportunity for stimulus and growth. Above all, she must reflect. Realizing that everything comes from and returns to God, she must help man perfect his talent for the enrichment, the joy, of all.

Granted her dedication to life in its fullness, granted the precedence of husband and children over all, if a woman is endowed, may she not still give something of herself to art? Of course she may, but in such a dual role the truly creative woman must be ready for disappointment and frustration. Something has to come out second-best, and the wise woman knows that it must not be her family. But she does know that some day her children will leave her, that her husband may be taken from her, and she does not extinguish her talent for lack of nourishment. She does learn that first things come first. For some it is a bitter lesson.

The chief enemy of the woman who essays that dual role is time—time and the luxury of continuity. From the instant when the "idea" first sparks to life in such a woman's spirit, until it is finally wrenched out of her, as a book, a painting, or whatever, her way is an obstacle course of unimportant yet urgent interruptions, the butcher, the baker, the baby, the thousand uninspiring clutterabilia of the household. All the while the idea is trying to find its own way out, crying insistently for the flesh it needs, growing not in quiet fluidity but in jerks and pauses and returns. The idea too often exhausts itself in the struggle for birth and arrives a corpse.

The forces of creativity are brutal and demanding, jealous of everything that does not bend to their urging, impetuous to claim every moment for themselves. Powerful and urgent they are nurtured on singleness of purpose, blind obedience to their insistence; put off, they become petulant; asked to compromise with time, frustrated; cross them at all and they wither and die, not for them the role of second love to be called forth when passion is spent, energies dissipated. And so the creative woman finds herself in a dilemma, asked to serve many masters, giving her all to none. Occasionally a woman follows the voice which tells her to forswear *all* for art.

Finally, there is that rare relationship of the husband who truly "husbands" his wife's creative energies, as Stieglitz did those of Georgia O'Keeffe, now in the front rank of American painters. Gentle Eugen Boissevain cherished and protected that delicate ivory tower of song, Edna St. Vincent Millay. Yet if children had graced those unions, all the care in the world could not have kept out the insistence of a small child's voice, the anxiety that comes with the job of motherhood.

As interpreter rather than creator of the arts, woman has had a smoother course. This is understandable, for she dances as a woman, acts as a woman, sings as a woman. However, there are notable exceptions. Isadora Duncan, in freeing the dance, was certainly more than an interpreter, was deeply creative. Following an unconventional pattern of life, she both bore three children and left the world a new and vital art form. On the other hand, the dedicated ballerina must deny herself the very heart of womanhood. Has anyone ever heard of a ballerina with five or six children? Actresses have been able to lead family lives, especially when their husbands shared the profession. Mme. Schumann-Heink raised seven children and still stood at the forefront of her field. Of course, her expansiveness, drive, and sheer physical stamina are not common. Like Duncan, she was an exception.

Today many doors are open for the woman in art—single women, women with time on their hands, women with vigorous years ahead, whose families are dispersed. The influence they can bring to the arts depends on the measure of woman they are.

For instance, more and more women are becoming critics of art and of literature. Many American newspapers are ill-equipped or not equipped at all to give their readers columns of art and literary criticism; yet it would be a genuine service to the community. Here woman's natural role as teacher and elevator of taste is called on to the full. She must discern and reject the merely fashionable, and, when necessary, have the courage to espouse the unpopular and the wit to explain the initially confusing.

Women are entering that still young profession, that of the museum director. Here is a rare opportunity for the total woman to emerge. Scholarship and a good eye she must have, but her skill as a housekeeper is no less important. She keeps the public home entrusted to her in shining order. Every painting, sculpture, antiquity and novelty must be placed to its best advantage, yet the over-all effect must seem effortless and pleasing. The woman museum director must be able to write well enough to make her treasures come alive for all, to make us see the fourteenth-century Virgin not on a pedestal in a marble gallery, but in her original habitat, a dim Gothic chapel whose doors open on to the valley of the Rhone. She must attract and intrigue the children of her community, encourage and instruct the young artist. Married or single, young or old, she is a mother in the full sense of the word.

Nor need a woman be a professional to influence life in her town for good in the arts. The woman with leisure has a whole spectrum of community efforts before her, all of which need her work and her heart and her voice. Choral and symphonic societies, record libraries, circulating art exhibits for hospitals and veterans' facilities, art programs for children, mobile libraries for rural districts—these are but a few of the worth-while activities depending, sometimes desperately, upon her good will and her good offices. The aura of beauty that glows in a well-run home can be projected to the whole city, which is, after all, a larger household.

The wise woman knows that her influence in a man's world can be limitless, but she knows she must exercise it as a woman, not as a competitor. The rare instances we have mentioned of the feminine "creator" only prove in their rarity that for most women the fullest creative realization comes as wife and mother. It is no less true in art than in politics, and it is no less true for being a truism, that the hand that rocks the cradle rules the world. Consider Vittoria Colonna, poet of the Italian Renaissance. Few read her poetry today, but her fruitful relationship with Michelangelo leaves all of us in her debt. He himself writes that she perfected his character as a sculptor perfects his clay model, "by carving it in hard, living stone."

Throughout history, woman has met the challenge implicit in her position with hope and courage, the courage of Empress Theodora who, when a mob threatened the palace and the

9

Emperor entreated that they flee, replied: "When nothing remains but safety in flight I say I will not fly. Those who have worn the crown should never survive its loss. Never shall I see the day when I shall no longer be called Empress. Caesar, it is well! The vessels are ready, the sea is open, but as for me, I remain."

Today there is a special urgency in the world's need for woman's work. The things of the spirit—woman's particular province—are threatened as never before by the dominance of materialism everywhere. The form in which it poses its most obvious threat is dialectical materialism, embodied in Soviet communism and dedicated to the destruction of the Christian culture which has been five thousand years abuilding. There is also a threat at home. The tremendous material achievements of the West have left us with a strong materialist bias ourselves; the increasing pressure of modern business life forces woman's man in the world into narrower channels of intense concentration upon exclusively material goals. Guided by the mass media, even children accept the materialist values, aims, and methods at an early age. Against these forces stands woman in the home, traditionally the gentle influence, the spiritual pole in the family.

Her primary weapon is love, enormously effective as a weapon precisely because she is incapable of using it as a weapon. At her disposal, as auxiliary tools, are all the arts of man and the age-old vision they forever renew of man as more than the beasts and only a little less than the angels.

We cannot reiterate too often the importance of the arts as an ally in the struggle of spirit against matter. Art, of its very nature, represents the intelligible union of spirit and matter. The artistic insight, however profound, does not really exist until the paint has been so arranged, the marble so hewn away, the bronze so cast, that the vision is recreated for the beholder. Art forces upon the beholder a disinterestedness that is rare in human activity. The painting or poem demands to be looked at for itself alone. When woman urges her husband and instructs

Chase Studios

FRANCES P. BOLTON

Ira L. Hill

ESTHER EBERSTADT BROOKE

PATRICIA CROWLEY

John Engstead

LILLIAN GISH

VALERIE HARVEY

JANE M. HOEY

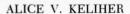

ALICE V. KELIHER

SISTER ELIZABETH KENNY

New York Times

ANNE O'HARE McCORMICK

Bradford Bachrach

MILLICENT C. McINTOSH

Marcus Blechman

ILONA MASSEY

Harris & Ewing

MARY T. NORTON

ELIZABETH RIDDER

MARION TURNER SHEEHAN

ELOISE SPAETH

HELEN C. WHITE

her children to go to art, she is leading them to contemplation, the highest spiritual state of human being.

By asking herself the questions suggested by these observations, and by looking at art for the answers, a woman can form her own mind in the appreciation of art and, having done so, place herself not as a boundary-marking frame of reference for her children's lives in art, but as a springboard. Art has survived ages darker than ours; through woman in the arts it will persist in its vital, spiritual role in our world.

II

ESTHER EBERSTADT BROOKE

Woman in Business and Management

SLOWLY but surely through the past several decades, there has been an ever increasing emphasis on the "value" of women in commercial enterprise. At first, to be sure, this dawning appreciation was little more than incredulous surprise as more and more women entered the white-collar field in a variety of clerical and stenographic-typing jobs, most of which they were discovered to perform with greater competence and stability than men ever did. To be sure, their importance was inconsequential, their presence shadowy, their highest aspirations no more than the "take-a-letter" level.

Little by little, however, the stature of this woman of business began to increase. From her vantage point of secondary importance, she absorbed both knowledge and added responsibilities. She became a sort of unofficial understudy whose observations were keen and objective, whose conclusions were logical and well drawn, and whose recommendations were worth listening to. In short, woman was so quietly but irrevocably insinuating herself into business as a vital and indispensable adjunct that when, suddenly, World War II burst upon us it was manifest that what had started as a trend had rolled into a tidal wave. The men were gone but the women were there—had been there all the time, in fact—and when trouser-clad women by the thousands began trooping into war plants, it was finally borne in on management that thousands of women in offices had also been "wearing the pants" for a long, long time.

As a nation we have always been more prodigal than thrifty, and I venture to say that had we wasted our natural resources as we have wasted our manpower, we would long since have been eating grass instead of spinach. So perhaps a major catastrophe was needed to force the issue of women's complete acceptance on the basis of ability alone. That women would eventually have received wholehearted recognition as one of our greatest hitherto untapped sources of production was inevitable. Inevitable, too, that, having competed with men in college, so many who had stood at the head of their class in school would be unwilling indefinitely to take a back seat in business. But it is significant that the new woman in business was temporarily willing to assume much the same role that since time immemorial she had occupied in the home; that in this new sphere of activity, instead of flaunting herself as a mental muscle man, she was content subtly to exercise her power from behind the throne until she was acknowledged as more than sufficiently equipped to grace the dais.

In the days of woman's novitiate as a business tycoon, many a militant feminist harped loudly and insistently upon "equality with men." Equality of hours, equality of pay. Equality of opportunity. Without, unfortunately, due consideration to the inequality of risk and the implicit inequality of hazard. Women, they maintained, could work like men, think like men, and should therefore be treated like men.

Others, who viewed the future of the working woman with more thoughtful regard, understood that woman could not possibly engage in shoulder to shoulder combat with men on the basis of equality. Neither was it a simple question of inferiority

13

on one side and superiority on the other. "Equality," which became the cornerstone of the fighting "women's righters," nearly became the stumbling block of women workers. Clearly, the essence of her dissimilarities to man account for some of woman's greatest compensations, her chief assets, and her major contributions to the world of work.

Man is strong; woman has stamina. Man is by nature deductive; woman intuitive. Man tends to plan in terms of the "broad progress"; woman excels at detail. Even her liabilities, properly assayed—like taking losses off your income tax—have played their inestimable part in raising the net universal profit calculable both in cash and comfort.

Woman's physical inferiority brought protective legislature, needed limitation of hours, safety measures, improved working conditions, and focused long overdue attention upon a need for many changes redounding to the benefit of employer and employee alike, regardless of sex. Far from being a deterrent to her progress in business, her sex could well be considered one of woman's most priceless [proprietary] properties.

By her very presence woman changes the entire atmosphere of an office. Was it W. & J. Sloane, those fine interior decorators, who banished the brass cuspidor and put carpets on the floor? It was not. It was quiet, ladylike, little Miss Janet who sat, notebook in hand, between the boss and the nearest baseboard. It was the growing army of well-behaved "little Miss Janets" who put a brake on the boss's tongue and ushered in a new era of business etiquette.

Not slow in their awareness of the value of woman, men soon began to capitalize on both her mental agility and her personal grace, until today it is axiomatic that women are not only a vital part of the business scene but of its scenery too. In other words, woman's entrance not only foreshadowed the end of man's monopolistic heredity but heralded the beginning of a major miracle in environment as well.

In sum, much of woman's intrinsic worth to business and to

14

many of the areas of work opportunity which she may exploit to her greatest advantage are hers not in spite of, but because of, her sex. It is often her "open sesame." It is always her responsibility, for she may employ it narrowly and selfishly as a lure, a weapon, a shield, a threat or shrewdly—yet unselfishly—as legitimate business equipment, vested solely in her, and with vast possibilities for the benefit of many.

What are some of these innate womanly characteristics and how may they be devoted to assure her progress in business? From civilization's earliest days, woman has been essentially domestic. At heart she is a homemaker with an unquenchable love of home and a deep pride in making the best of her surroundings. The average woman is an efficient housekeeper, always on the alert for more effective means to expedite her work, save time and effort, get the most for her money. She improvises work schedules, devises kitchen aids, avoids using three of anything where two would suffice.

This age-old concept of system and order found a fertile field in commerce and industry, where all those basic talents are readily adapted as a whole or a part of the effective performance of widely assorted tasks. To point to but a few of the more obvious, tailor-made opportunities—obvious because one scarcely ever sees a man there today—woman was a natural at the clerical desk, in the file room, in the library.

Not because clerical work is a sedentary task and she was weary of walking did woman find herself at the desk, but because business appreciates her steadfastness in the face of routine and she, bright creature, sensed an enlarging sphere of activity as she boiled down that routine.

Not because she had nimble fingers, knew how to open and shut bureau drawers, or drop knives, forks, and spoons into their allotted slots was woman soon called a "born file executive," but because she *is* a born coordinator of things and ideas and because, after centuries of carrying around in the active file above her ears the classified confidences of her spouse, man-in-

15

the-plural instinctively trusted her with the same type of business responsibility.

Not by accident did woman drift into the library but because books were her main source of education, often her greatest inspiration, her source of information, and because in the public library as in the commercial library she gained while giving. To the library she brought the distilled experience of time-honored women who had helped tiny hands to turn the colored page, who had slowly led growing minds to thirst for the magic of the written word and to enjoy the challenging pursuit of the uncompleted.

From these three primary beginnings the woman in the white-collar world went racing down innumerable broad career highways and tiptoed along countless exploratory bypaths until today there is scarcely a field which she cannot prepare to enter.

We are not here concerned with the broad areas of woman's work, the fields within those areas which may be greenest, nor what is needed to open these fields to new entrants. That is a digression which deserves its own special attention.

Our concentration is upon a few of the spots currently occupied by woman and how she may, perhaps, perpetuate herself in those places and extend her influence.

The word "secretary" today invariably brings to mind a young woman—practically never a man. But no longer is the secretary the convenient dumping ground for someone's uncontrolled temper, the submissive recipient of unprovoked verbal barrages once reserved strictly for men of affairs with inferiority complexes at home. Today's secretary has inherited lavishly from the dignified forbearance of her predecessor, the impact of whose personality made boots on the desk an anachronism and whose demonstrated acumen brought business to its feet in admiration.

The legacy of the secretary of today is a title that is often a misnomer, a job whose scope is limitless, an opportunity as apprentice to the master minds who control and direct the wheels of progress. Underlying [this legacy] is an open bid to quit as a back-seat driver and take the wheel.

One creaky relic of the didies-not-dollars-for-women era is the deathless myth that women hate figures. The truth is that woman brought to business an orderly mind, trained by years of battling with the budget. Woman is the only creature on earth able to multiply nothing by nothing and get something out of it. She is inherently a bookkeeper with an accountant's delight in the profit column and a determined broom to sweep away the loss.

The woman accountant holds one of the most important places business has to offer. She must be highly skilled after her years of training and, in addition, she must be possessed of a marked degree of discretion and honor. For hers is a position of trust. Affairs of the greatest importance and of the most confidential nature are placed in her hands. She is a "key man" in a pivotal cynosure which she may use as a stepping stone in a variety of directions. Great is the accountants's responsibility—to herself, to her company, and to her conscience. She is more than a recorder of the *fait accompli;* she must often be the sentinel and safeguard of rectitude.

Out of this welter of working women emerged another member of the dramatis personae, again forceful because of her inborn personality traits. At first replacing the superannuated pensioner or the incompetent in-law, woman came into her own as a first-rate personnel executive. What better sphere for the maternal instinct to care for and protect? for tolerance and understanding? for the just peacemaker? for the honorable negotiator? for the practical guide and counselor? Here was a need for someone with imagination and ability to interpret job demands in terms of the properly qualified human being and to translate human needs and aspirations in terms of the right job.

The woman personnel director answered that crying need to which none but a woman could have brought her combination of mental, emotional, and psychological equipment.

Women did not blunder into these or any other business careers purely by accident. *Men* first put them there because *men* perceived woman's singular qualifications. However, with all due respect for his transcendent astuteness, man, as usual with his eyes on the horizon, overlooked the obvious. One of the greatest spurs to ambition is to be underestimated. So woman occupies her significant place in business today largely because, through dogged determination, she burst the bonds of man's preconceived notions of the limits of her capacities.

Mary Dillon, for example, was quick to perceive that open invitation and receptive to its implications. Starting work at seventeen, she rose to become the first woman president of a public utility in this country—an important corporation which she ran with all the proficiency of the men by whom she had been tutored, plus her own inherent grace that was no mean asset to her company.

Granted, this may be an exception. It is the exception that proves the rule—proves two rules in fact. In the first place it proves that the right woman with the right attributes *can* move to the top and, in the second place, that she need not resort to ruthlessness nor sacrifice her femininity in so doing.

In the competitive climate of free enterprise, woman's ingenuity has been quick to contrive time- and money-saving short-cuts and to substitute for the inertia of desultory efforts the smooth flow of properly channeled work. The "clerk" of yesterday is the supervisor—the executive—of today, responsible for the quantity and the quality of what is done by her group.

Less evident but more profound and more peremptory is a further responsibility which is at once the privilege, the duty, and the challenge of every right-thinking woman now in business.

Working side-by-side with men, particularly during the past quarter of a century, women have participated in an era of material progress that beggars description. The whole world looks with envious eyes at our seemingly endless wealth of opportunity, our unceasing forward strides as field after field opens up, spreads out, and prospers. With lightning speed the dreams of the drafting board seem to be absorbed into acceptance on a par with the electric icebox or the vacuum sweeper; communication by radio, already outdistanced by radar; the commercial practicability of television while an industry scarcely out of the cradle.

Working at her office job, woman has made her own contribution to the long list of our amazing feats of material progress: electronics, that mysterious and complicated science which performs whole catalogues of new wonders from opening doors without hands to cooking steaks without heat or smoke; railroads with princely appointments; air speeds faster than sound. While simultaneously, woman chemists and physicists have been helping literally to remake material itself, fashioning it anew for greater service to mankind, so that daily we reap the benefit of chemical research and development applied directly to improved living conditions and to making this a much better world *in a material sense*.

To the sober woman in her hard-won, supervisory capacity, appraising with justifiable pride this quarter century during which she "came of age" as a bona fide executive, one fact of great significance stands out raw and bare and ugly. Our truly magnificent *material* attainments have not been even closely approached by any corresponding emphasis on exploring or satisfying our *spiritual* needs.

In 1932 the youth of our nation were beguiled with glittering promises of lustrous work opportunities. Their pliant minds were subjected to a type of thought direction new in the annals of American history—the live-off-the-other-fellow approach to success. A moral fog began drifting across the nation to blanket our schools, mildew our books, dampen and loosen the joints of our home units. Furthermore, the spectacle of corruption in government, the open betrayal of trust by public servants, the frankly

The Spiritual Woman

Communist influence in many quarters tended to taint the thinking of our young people and color their morals.

Soberly, in 1952, a troubled nation reviewed many past political promises of which two of the most captivating—"opportunity" without honest labor, ease without thrift—had boomeranged into vitiated ambition, had invited laziness and cheating, and had fostered lawlessness under government subsidy. The biggest crime wave and the largest number of juvenile delinquents in our history were in part the result of deliberate and vicious destruction of the fine principles of spiritual uprightness inherited from our God-fearing founding fathers. American youth may have been given unprecedented opportunity, as promised, but after twenty years it seemed more a chance at crime than at a career or a craft.

Soberly, today, the woman executive surveys the effect of these years on the thinking and bearing of her subordinates. She is conscious of a new solemnity and a new compulsion, for now there is laid upon her the responsibility for imbuing her young associates with *wholesome attitudes,* with *meritorious loyalties,* and with *integrity of purpose.* The clock-watcher, the time-stealer, the malingerer are one and all her charges, and the woman who seizes this challenge as one of her larger career opportunities, instead of succumbing to the temptation to complain, dismiss, or quit, is the indispensable woman in business.

To put it another way, one of woman's greatest opportunities in business today is not her chance to crack the sound wall of the dollar area, which—in large measure—she has already done, but the hope of success in a far more important sphere of influence as preceptor and mentor of our future business leaders. That woman has picked up this gauntlet flung in her path by time and circumstance is becoming everywhere evident.

We hear reference on all sides to the "power of woman." What does it mean? It means that—welcome or not—woman is a spiritual powerhouse just going into big-scale production for the good of our homes, our business, and our country. It means that more and more women must—and will—awake to their moral obligation to contribute actively rather than passively to the world.

The supervisor must inculcate a high standard of decency and ethics into her staff. The librarian must make available material that strengthens rather than subverts the inquiring mind. The personnel director, more than ever mindful of the human element, must administer rules and regulations to the mutual benefit of both employer and employee.

On the policy-making level, the personnel director must increasingly work with unflagging persistence to hasten the day when each man, *in accordance with his mental and social equipment,* may enjoy *social* as well as *political* equality with his fellow man of like capacities. When he slinks into a back seat only because *he disgraced himself* and not because of anyone's preconceptions, predilections, or prejudices. In this new dawn of "spiritual democracy," her selection of new employees can no longer be made on personal preference but thoughtfully, conscientiously, on the basis of fitness—both mental and moral—to perform a given task.

The resolute administrator of today puts new emphasis on the training and indoctrination programs that are a part of her duties. As a good housekeeper she brings with her an abhorrence of waste in time and material. She is insistent on ending overlapping, interlocking, and deadlocking, at once so crippling and so costly. Moreover, she is on the alert to pattern and to impart constructive habits of doing and thinking that develop a strong center of poise within the heart and clean the mind of destructive, corroding isms.

This awakened conscience of the few *must* be made to communicate itself to the minds, the imaginations, and the consciences of *all* women in administrative capacities so that the small, whispered beginnings of spiritual values in the material world may swell to the crescendo of a trumpet call that will not be denied.

The Spiritual Woman

Whether she finds herself "in business" on the government payroll or on that of private enterprise, the contemporary woman in management can no longer tolerate the slow poison of *laissez faire*. The still, small voice must be anything but stilled in her. She has much to say and must dare to say it with dignity and with telling *suavité*.

Conscience, in truth, has never made a coward of woman. This new compulsion of hers, this gathering, cumulative energy may well be defined as the result of a united, articulate, driving force for high principles—a fresh and vitalizing source of strength wherever woman may choose to employ it.

Man, by himself, has satisfied our material aspirations with a *material* prosperity beyond our ambitions and unequaled in the history of the world. It would be folly for woman to presume to put herself in a class with such "know-how." She may be more brilliant than the greatest genius among men, but *only one thing can she contribute* which is hers alone to give—a spiritual infusion, *distinctively feminine*. A spiritual infusion necessary to enrich the bloodstream of mankind's thinking, contaminated as it has been by too great a preoccupation with material success. Immeasurable riches, uniquely her own, to add to what man might otherwise have completed with only sterile efficiency.

This infusion of her gentility, this spiritual power of her personality, should, above all else, be the working woman's chief bequest to what was once accepted as a man's world.

Management's new woman, aroused by the frightening consequences of spreading materialism, is determined that this shall be done. Her job—wherever it is, whatever it is—has a new dimension reaching toward the soul and facing new horizons of ascendant strength.

But, though eager to press forward with men to greater heights, management's new woman is no longer deceived by old clichés or half-truths, for she knows now that advancement is not always synonymous with progress. She has seen integrity and virtue too long shelved among the rusting remains of discredited philosophies and she knows now that it is imperative that woman draft new designs of propriety and blaze new trails of ethical conduct. And driven by a new resolve and firm conviction, she knows now that she must be ever more determined to bend her might to the end that henceforth our spiritual progress shall keep abreast of our material growth.

In this disruptive era of uncertain national prestige, of dwindling personal integrity, woman's greatest challenge—nay, her irrevocable trust—is to rebuild the spiritual foundation on which America's greatness rests. With the unique persistence, the power, the poise, and the personal responsibility which have ever been her distinguishing feature.

Epochs and eras always seem to coin their own catch phrases and slogans. Perhaps the punch line of tomorrow will be that management's buried treasure was the released spiritual power of woman today; that she brought to the ailing world of unstable, material currencies the lasting and untarnishable coin of spiritual wealth.

III

ALICE V. KELIHER

Woman and Media of Communication

THE powerful influence of mass media has been demonstrated again and again in our times. We have witnessed the horror caused by dictators with their propaganda machines and the devilish cleverness with which they have been able to use the mass media to distort people's minds and feelings. We should know by now the power of the "big lie oft repeated." We should not let ourselves forget the forfeit of six million Jews due to the mass mesmerizing of Germans who might otherwise have been God-fearing, family-loving, decent persons.

Mechanization and the anesthetizing of feelings are great challenges of our times. The sense of impotence as an individual in the face of vast power is prevalent. Yet this insecurity grows out of man-made power, whereas the primitive felt helpless in the face of the natural phenomena of wind, storm, drought, and death.

Are the mass media of radio and television aware of their great potential? Are women—housewives, mothers, daughters, sisters, "career girls"—aware of what influence these media have on them and on their families?

"Can someone use some influence to get the TV show that is on between five and six in the evening changed? It frightens my six-year-old girl to death."

"My boy has his radio on from the time he wakes up until he goes to sleep, and sometimes after, for I often have to turn it off for him. He has it on while he studies and when he seems to be reading. I wonder if he is really listening. What *can* I do about it?"

Many parents have yielded their authority to the insistent attraction of these mass media. Many admit frankly that they cannot turn off the TV set when the child insists on seeing a show. Many have yielded to the point of serving supper on trays in front of the TV set. One mother excuses this breakdown of the family-at-dinner-together unity by saying, "Now my boy eats everything I put on his tray if he can watch TV while he eats." Another mother frankly admits that the TV set mesmerized her eight-year-old boy and served as a useful "baby sitter."

A degree of this parental irresponsibility is at the root of our juvenile problem. But press, radio, television, and moving pictures are not thereby exonerated from all guilt. An entertainer was banned from TV for experimenting with a kiss estimated variously at two to five minutes in length. Happily large numbers of the TV audience protested. The feeble defense of the male entertainer who was involved was that his wife was present! The ideas and ideals implanted in the minds of young people by decent parents meet severe competition from such a display!

In 1954 close to sixty million people watched *I Love Lucy* every Monday night. Eisenhower was elected President of the United States by fewer people. Undoubtedly between seventy and eighty million Americans watch television each week. As more stations are added and more sets purchased the number is increasing.

Our deepest concern is about the effects on children and youth of the obsessional preoccupation with such ready-made entertainment. What is happening to the creative activities of our boys and girls? What of their vigorous outdoor life and sports? Are we developing a passive population? What of the dangerous implications of letting the other fellow do it?

In 1950, Paul Witty [1] found that children with TV sets in their own homes averaged 3.13 hours of viewing each day. The six-year-olds averaged 2.85 per day! Other surveys place child viewing as high as 27 hours a week. Fred M. Hechinger said in November 1952:

But it is appalling that over a full week sixth and seventh graders were found to spend thirty non-school hours watching television as compared with twenty-five hours spent in school. More than half of these children were permitted to watch any programs they chose, and 86 per cent chose Milton Berle first, followed by "Six Gun Theater." . . .[2]

Statistics on child and adult viewing will be invalid the week after this chapter is printed. However, the pace of development of this newest, and undoubtedly most powerful, of the mass media suggests the problem created for the American family in learning how to live with it and to control its power wisely. The speed with which TV is growing creates critical problems for the station owner and program producer as well. With the many hours to fill there is serious question as to whether we have enough creative people aware of the scope and possibilities of TV to produce worth-while material. The medium seems to have grown faster than the available talent.

Television was first authorized on a commercial basis five months before Pearl Harbor. At the end of World War II there were six television stations on the air. By January 1950 there were 98. . . . When the war ended, there were 7,000 receiving sets in the entire country; in early 1950 the number exceeded 4 million.[3]

[1] Paul Witty, "Children's, Parents' and Teachers' Reactions to Television," *Elementary English*, Vol. XXVII, October 1950, Number 6, pp. 349–396.
[2] New York *Herald Tribune*, November 8, 1952.
[3] Siepmann, Charles, *Radio, Television and Society*, Oxford University Press, 1950, p. 318.

Charles Siepmann says of TV, "To point at it is like pointing at a jet plane—it has passed out of sight while you raised an astonished finger." [4]

As compared with 1950's 98 stations, 1954 had 360 in operation. In 1951 the number of receiving sets passed the ten-million mark and six months later was estimated to be twelve million. Seven thousand to nineteen million sets in less than a decade indicates the pace with which the American public is turning to TV. As this chapter goes to press, we learn that there are 34,364,000 sets. With this speedier-than-mushroom growth of the industry the mother who asked what could be done about the show that terrified her child might well give pause and ask just what her child's future interests are likely to be. Leaders in the industry realize that there is serious question about the quality of material seen by America's families—particularly its children.

Proof of the positive concern for wholesome fare is the two-hour production of Peter Pan and the repetitions from time to time of *Amahl and the Night Visitors,* an exquisite spiritual contribution first commissioned for TV presentation.

Weeks spent monitoring shows for children had notable bright spots—*Ding Dong School,* Ireene Wicker, *The Big Top,* Charity Bailey, *Mr. Wizard, Through the Enchanted Gate, Kukla, Fran and Ollie, Disneyland,* etc. But far too many programs designed for children exploit them. There seem to be two typical patterns. A man in Western clothes sits with a group of children (who are often more interested in waving at parents and audience than in the movie) and views with them some old movie. In one case it was a rather harrowing old version of Pocahontas. The second pattern is using child performers who vary from tots gyrating in bewilderment to pre-professional youngsters in a variety and dance show. One dance studio offered a five-dollar gift certificate and a guarantee that the child would appear before television. How many children may thus be sacrificed on the altar of parental ambition?

[4] *Ibid.,* p. 317.

Indeed, as one travels about the nation, to communities remote from sending stations, the typical sight is of a huge TV antenna outfit pinned to the earth with numerous guy wires and crouched under it, looking apologetic, a house. The engineers who install antennas say that there are more than fifteen million of some size or shape poised on rooftops of American homes.

This sharpens the question of what comes into American homes. Today, children two years old and less know how to flip the switch that turns on the magic pictures and sounds. As in the early days of motion pictures and comics, the TV industry realizes the need for self-regulation and is working on it. There has been improvement but still there is too much *double-entendre,* allusion to sex, low neckline, crime content, leering at pretty girls. And let us not forget that the old Westerns before which children sit with riveted attention for several hours at a time are not innocent of the above violations of good taste just because they are old. Many of them contain dubious material for child viewing.

The designing of TV programs for children should be given much more attention. The phenomenal success of "Miss Frances" of *Ding Dong School* undoubtedly grows out of her knowledge of children, her determination to serve them well, the wisdom of her producers and advisers, and a deep sense of integrity.

We could say the same for Ireene Wicker, Charity Bailey, Bert Tillstrom, Fran Ellison, Victor D'Amico, and others who have made real efforts to serve the needs of children. But the fact that a few programs are designed for children does not relieve the TV industry of its responsibility for the general caliber of material seen by boys and girls.

In Witty's 1950 study, children's preferences were: Hopalong Cassidy, *Howdy Doody, The Lone Ranger,* Milton Berle, Arthur Godfrey, *Small Fry,* Sports, *Kukla, Fran and Ollie.* The popularity of Berle and Godfrey with *children* should have given them pause in 1950. They might then have tested the legend that Americans have juvenile minds. The latest Witty studies show that *I Love Lucy* has outpaced all other shows with children of all ages. There was a time when P.T.A.'s and civic groups avoided "Uncle Miltie's" Tuesday night hour for meetings. Now the harmless and often riotous doings of Lucy's family seem to hold sway. Could it be that children, unspoiled by falseness, are responsible for this switch? If so, thanks should be proffered to them by putting *I Love Lucy* on at an earlier hour so they will not have to slumber in school on Tuesdays.

Professors Dallas Smythe of the University of Illinois and Donald Horton of the University of Chicago made a survey of TV programs offered in the New York area for one week, in January 1951. They reported such results as:

Out of 564 hours of programming during the week, 57 hours were devoted to crime dramas.

An additional 44 hours were devoted to "Westerns"—chiefly crime drama on horseback. Substantially all of the Westerns, of course, were Hollywood films—as were many of the crime dramas.

As early as 1950 Hollywood's production for TV outnumbered its presentations for movie theaters. Continuing the survey,

More than 37 hours were devoted to "quizzes, stunts, and contests." A large portion of these—nearly 16 hours—were "telephone shows," in which viewers at home are telephoned and given a chance to win a prize.

More than 76 hours were devoted to vaudeville and variety shows.

Of those 564 program hours on seven New York TV stations, only an hour and a quarter was devoted to serious music programs. *Exactly half an hour went for fine arts programs.* More than 30 per cent of all children's programs were Westerns and thrillers. Westerns were classified as "for children" if they appeared between 5 and 7 P.M. or if they were introduced as "for the kiddies."

During 1950 the average television station devoted only 0.9 per cent of its time to religion and 3 per cent to education. Wayne Coy, then Chairman of F.C.C. reported this to a meeting of the National Association of Radio and Television Broadcasters. "It is clear," he said, "that some steps must be taken by broadcasters to discover what the needs of their communities really are."

But where is the listening and viewing public? Where are the women who hold so much influence in the development of our society? Mr. Coy reported that during a *seventy-two-day period,* in 1950, there were only one thousand complaints against TV. They included concerns about indecency, obscenity, advertising of alcoholic beverages, crime and horror, excessive advertising, fortune telling, and attacks on religious faiths. There were then some millions of sets in operation, but only a thousand protests. Are we becoming passive?

With, apparently, an aching conscience, Dr. Lee De Forest, inventor of the three-element vacuum tube, said that "his grandchild, television, was running wild." In 1951 he said:

Television, which could be so uplifting and enlightening, is being used degradingly. In Los Angeles, where I live, there are eighty or ninety murders a week broadcast on television programs, mostly movies. This is alarming, wicked and must not be tolerated forever. It can only have a vicious effect on children. Sponsors must reform and raise their intellectual levels. And I honestly believe they could do it if they would act together, without losing a single viewer.[5]

Dr. De Forest's alarm is shared by Charles Seipmann, Director of the Communications Center at New York University's School of Education. He expresses his concern in a letter to this writer.

For me the significance of television in the social sense is powerful and terrifying in one respect above all others. Radio captured the imagination of the preadolescent child (*The Lone Ranger, Superman,* etc.). Television has gone one better and embraces the child world right down to about the four-year level. It is scarcely an exaggeration to say that child development today proceeds from suckling to weaning to television viewing. What the consequences are we do not know but what is full of terrifying impact is the fact that mass communication has now become a force that literally influences from the cradle to the grave.

Much thought must be given by American mothers to the meaning of all this. They and their children must not become a "captive audience." They are not compelled to look and listen.

[5] *The New York Times,* June 10, 1951.

Neither must they stay up past reasonable bedtime hours if parents have convictions about what is good for their children and then live by these convictions. A big overstuffed chair, or a rocking chair with Mother's lap or arm available, and a story book, would provide powerful competition with a TV show that can frighten children. No TV show within the reach of imagination could be as attractive as companionship with a beloved mother and a good book.

Many librarians have worked toward connecting interest in TV shows with book reading. Some report that they have increased the use of books connected with TV themes. Others are pessimistic about the fact that one cannot read and look at TV at the same time. Jack Gould's survey in June 1951 showed that "sale of books to adults has fallen off in most cities, but public libraries report an upward trend in the lending of books. Rental libraries in retail stores report a decline ascribed to both television and competition from 25-cent books sold in drugstores and newsstands." The specific reports Gould collected from various cities, however, indicated that reading has dropped off in many and increased in others. He confirmed the findings of some of the librarians, "One consistent trend that apparently affects all types of reading matter is how closely it resembles the program material available on video." [6]

This is not surprising in that tastes dictate choices in both fields. But the development of more mature tastes is an educational task to be shared mutually by the family, the TV producer, and the school. Fifty years ago, John Dewey said that a child could want only the best he has ever known. If the home introduces the child early to good books, music, storytelling, adventure, doing and making things together; if the school echoes and extends this by giving the child rich and fine choices in literature, dramatics, science experiences, and the arts—then standards are being built and boys and girls are learning to distinguish the beautiful from the cheap and vulgar. TV production must and

[6] *The New York Times,* June 14, 1951.

31

will follow, for the ear is always to the ground and what the public demands it gets. It behooves parents to see the shows their children see, know what is in them, talk them over, make choices together of what is really good, and then kindly but firmly stick to an agreed-upon schedule.

Perhaps the most vulnerable children are those who have no supervision of what they see and hear, for whom the TV set actually becomes the "baby sitter." Far too many children have no help in deciding what to turn on—what the actual choices are. Too often Mother is not home when children return from school. Or, if she is, she is busy about household tasks, preparing dinner, and is frankly relieved to have the children quietly occupied with TV even if the show is an old Western, "crime on horseback."

An unpublished survey of 87 children in a metropolitan school revealed that 36 of the 87 chose their own programs with no supervision whatsoever. Of these fourth-, fifth-, and sixth-grade children, 31 said that they and their parents together made the selections. The study did not inquire into how well they stuck to these mutually arrived at selections.[7]

Another problem was indicated, though it was not the central part of the inquiry, and that is that children stay up later than they should to see certain popular night shows with their parents. Most of us can remember how, as children, we hated to go to bed when anything was "going on," when there was interesting company, we wanted to be in on it. Perhaps today's child wants equally to share his parents' interests, conversations, activities. If begging to stay up for "just this one show" means companionship with Mother and Father, then it is quite possible that the child's choice of preferred shows has more to do with companionship than it does with the content of the offering. This could be one poignant reason why shows clearly designed for adults and pre-sumably too sophisticated for children appear so often near or at the top of their choices of favorites. Today's parents, confused by

[7] Unpublished study by Mrs. Adele Weiss, graduate student at New York University's School of Education.

the demands made on them, fail to realize how important their companionship is to children, how deeply and at times desperately the child wants to see his parents happily together, wants to share in that togetherness for the certainty of belonging. If Father really knew how much his thirteen-year-old daughter wanted to read her last awkward essay to him, he would turn off the newscast, knowing there would be a later one, and give his undivided attention to her. Or his eleven-year-old son, just entering Junior High School, is worried that he is not as tall as the others and wants to talk to Dad about it. Maybe the six-year-old, with the missing front teeth, wants to tell about the circus her group gave and the funny false teeth she invented so she could be a tigress. Far too often Mother or Father will say something like, "That will have to wait. I can't miss this show." So the child waits, grows to think of the the show as the way of being bound to parents. Then the requests come to stay up just a little later.

Teachers are quite aware of what the extra staying-up hours mean for the next day. One first-grade teacher who follows the happy practice of sending notes home whenever anything important happens—the gay events, the firsts, the accomplishments, the needs for drying wet feet, for watching the reddening nose—sent the following.

Dear Mrs. Jones,

Susan told us all about *I Love Lucy* today and did a beautiful job of making us love their baby, too.

But later she got very tired and sleepy. I hope you will help her get off to bed earlier tonight.

Thank you,

Miss Teacher

The invention of TV is part of the progress of our times. We would be more than foolish to say that we should discard such a useful device. All who learn from Congressional hearings, those who enjoy World Series baseball games, who follow the filmed news, and the fair and balanced opinion shows on TV are grateful for the use to which intelligent leaders are putting this powerful medium. If there be fault, it is not in the mechanical medium, but in the people who use it for production and for consumption.

We must, in fairness, thank TV for what it does to give comfort to the shut-in, the crippled, the aged, and those who are too far removed from world events to keep up with them as well as they are shown on TV. We repeat, the invention, the instrumentality itself, cannot be blamed for the lack of creative talent which guides its use, nor the values implicit in its general content. It is only fair to say that there is much more awareness of what is happening in the world and in the nation because of the coverage faithfully given by television.

And yet, as we go to press, how could it be that the National Association for Better Radio and TV reported that in Los Angeles there were four times as many filmed TV programs based on crime and violence as three years before? If the American public gets what it asks for, what does this mean?

Just as TV is undergoing rapid changes due to its speed of development, radio listening is changing. Evening radio listening is the most affected. This is logical. Daytime radio which can be heard while household tasks are performed retains its popularity. Evening and night programs which compete with free hours for TV are suffering noticeably, so much so that rates for a broadcasting hour at times that used to be very expensive have dropped 10 to 15 per cent. Hooper ratings for shows which used to have top popularity have dropped in some cases more than 75 per cent. All have dropped more than 50 per cent. This is another way of saying that writing about radio is like writing in swift-moving water and one may only point to trends and to the lasting appeal of certain types of radio.

With all of the decline in evening and night radio listening, the daytime serial, or "soap opera," seems to be holding its largely female audience. The best estimates we can secure indicate that at least twenty million women listen to serials each weekday. These "soap operas," so named because most of them advertise some brand of soap, soap powder, flakes, or liquid cleanser, are an amazing phenomenon of American life. They have had an unbelievable grip on women of all walks of life and all degrees of education. Script writers have been hard put to it to resolve long-continuing plots as much as seventeen years on the same serial without letting any characters grow older or die. Women have timed their marketing, their visiting of sick neighbors, and their hospitality to callers, by their favorite serials. Letters to sponsors warn of boycotts of their products if favorite characters meet with undue difficulty or disaster. Most important of all, as we shall mention later, women find their solutions for their own human relations problems in these 13½-minute scripts which succeed each other over the air without a break for hours at a time.

In 1954, a New York City woman, on a Monday, could listen to serials from 10:45 A.M. with few intermissions until 6:00 P.M.

> *When a Girl Marries,* ABC 10:45
> *Rosemary,* CBS 11:45
> *Aunt Jenny,* CBS 12:15
> * *Helen Trent,* CBS 12:30
> * *Our Gal Sunday,* CBS 12:45
> * *Ma Perkins,* CBS 1:15
> * *Young Dr. Malone,* CBS 1:30
> * *The Guiding Light,* CBS 1:45
> *Second Mrs. Barton,* CBS 2:00
> *Perry Mason,* CBS 2:15
> *This Is Nora Drake,* CBS 2:30
> *The Brighter Day,* CBS 2:45
> * *Hilltop House,* CBS 3:00
> * *Life Can Be Beautiful,* NBC 3:00
> * *Road of Life,* NBC 3:15
> * *Pepper Young's Family,* NBC 3:30
> * *Right to Happiness,* NBC 3:45
> * *Backstage Wife,* NBC 4:00
> * *Stella Dallas,* NBC 4:15
> * *Young Widder Brown,* NBC 4:30

The Spiritual Woman

Woman in My House, NBC 4:45
° *Just Plain Bill,* NBC 5:00
Front Page Farrell, NBC 5:15
° *Lorenzo Jones,* NBC 5:30 [8]

At this writing it is impossible to know what is happening to radio listening. Many of the serials have moved from radio to TV. Others have maintained their honorable place (*Pepper Young's Family* for seventeen years; *Dr. Christian* for fifteen years) in the devotion of listeners who have from time to time found help with their human problems. More often, we fear, radio serials have presented unreal and sentimental solutions to life's problems—witness the series in which the star has been "over thirty-five" for at least thirteen years, succeeding in attracting young men of talent, fame, and wealth, to prove that one can be attractive after thirty-five!

The serious implication for American wives and mothers is that far too often the solution of the daytime serial has seemed to have validity for helping them to solve their problems. Women have been known to say, "If somebody asks me for advice I listen to Helen Trent, or I tell my friend to listen to her. That's where you find out what to do when you have a problem." Even if we grant that the script writer may have excellent insight for the play he is creating and the characters he is delineating, he would be the last one to claim that his characters have found general solutions for the cares of all American women.

It has often been said that we Americans are becoming spectators, not doers, in our recreational lives. This was said in the early days of the movies. It can truly be said of today's fixation with 34 million TV sets. Is this the fault of the mechanical instrument known as television or radio? Or is it the problem of a vacuum in American family life in which companionship, doing things together, and sharing of interests has reached such

[8] The serials with asterisks have been on the air ten years or more. *Portia Faces Life* has been on for ten years but was not in the New York City offering listed above.

a low ebb that empty time encourages the riveted attention to mechanical means no matter what the content? When the eight-year-old comes home from school and sits for three hours before old Westerns, is it the vital attraction of the medium, or the absence of backyard playmates, apples and cookies, fascinating story books, Mother or Grandmother with old-time stories to tell?

The basic challenge is to American family life. Any mechanical distraction strong enough to take one fourth to one fifth of a child's waking hours away from the human beings he should love and cherish must challenge the depth of devotion and keenness of interest in those relationships. We need a renascence of interest in and concern for the development of our children, development in which, we pray, we adults may have values of rich spiritual depth to offer that we will not feel threatened by the valuable mechanical instruments we have discovered, but will find the ways to use them for human welfare and development.

This calls for constant communication. The public, parents in particular, must be alert and active in communicating with station owners, sponsors, and the F.C.C.[9] about the programs that are *good* as well as those that are *bad*. In a deep sense America's values are at stake.

[9] Federal Communications Commission, Washington, D. C.

IV

ILONA MASSEY

Woman and Communism

I T IS always hard for people in a free country to realize what conditions are like behind the Iron Curtain. I did not fully realize what was happening in the beautiful country of my birth until 1947, when my mother arrived in the United States from Hungary, a country enslaved first by the Nazis and now by the Communists. Her personal accounts strengthen my conviction that communism is a system which is opposed to what I believe. Before I heard this firsthand information from my mother, I was not actively interested in politics and systems. I can recall a happy family life in Hungary where, at an early age, I was attracted to the stage.

After my mother's arrival in the United States, I began to take an active part against communism at every opportunity, despite the usual threats from Soviet agents in this country to many of us who speak out publicly against the Communist system. In 1948, the Hungarian Communist Government offered me a leading role in the theater if I would return. I was told that all my expenses would be paid and promised a fabulous sum for my public appearance and acceptance of the present Communist regime. I turned down the offer and I still receive the threats.

Woman and Communism

It was natural for my friends in this country, foreign and American born, to ask my mother about conditions under the Communist system. Is it true that laborers are severely punished when they are late for work? My mother confirmed this and other happenings which my friends took with a grain of salt, hardly believing that such atrocities could occur at the slightest infraction of rules. I am convinced that one of the greatest aids to the cause of communism is the unrealistic habit of those who do not believe the lengths to which this system will go to enforce domination over human beings. If we never experience the pangs of hunger, it is difficult to know what hunger is. It is a blessing that America has not had to suffer occupation by the Nazis and the Communists. The atrocities inflicted upon innocent people are hard to imagine. Only now and then, a specific case in an occupied country comes to light and arouses public indignation.

It borders on a miracle for anyone to secure a visa to get out of the Communist countries. It might be difficult for some to believe but when those who are fortunate enough to obtain a visa are handed those wonderful papers, the very officer handing them to the lucky individual finds a way to whisper in her ear, "Don't forget to tell the free world what we are going through here . . . what is happening to us . . . tell them everything!" Yet, today, this whispering does not have quite the same hopefulness as even three years ago, because now to the whisper is added, ". . . tell them everything, even if they will not believe it!" How can free people imagine, for instance, that in Hungary today, the tattoo business is a flourishing one!

The desperate need for tattoo began in Budapest when the government started deportations and forced separation of children from parents. The grief-stricken parents managed to have a tattoo mark placed on the child's arm. A similar mark was made on the mother's arm so that both mother and child would bear the same tattooed marking. Sometimes it was a code giving place and date of birth; other times it was a special marking known only to the family. This was done before the children were

39

forcibly collected and taken to the Mathias Rakosi, a home for children where they are brought up as wards of the government and indoctrinated with Communist philosophy. Any recollection of parents is systematically erased from the child's memory. He is taught to deny God and to obey the government system. Even the children of parents selected for military service or labor groups are sent to Mathias Rakosi. These parents are forced to sign papers agreeing to the surrender of parental rights to this Communist government-run institution. Parents know that their child will be given another name and his previous records destroyed. It is heartening that in the sign of the tattoo these parents show a symbol of faith and hope that some day family unity will be restored even in the face of these anti-God practices; that at some time, the weight of the strong-arm behind the Iron Curtain will be lifted and families will once again live together in freedom.

One of the most diabolical schemes in Hungary that profoundly shocked my mother was the Communist technique of using children to spy on parents. One important ray of hope for those behind the Iron Curtain is the radio. Parents who are fortunate enough to be able to hide their radios from confiscation guard them with their lives because through this instrument they are able to listen to the Voice of America and the free world. The teachers in Hungary are forced to find out from small pupils if their parents own a radio. They trick the innocent child into betraying his parents by asking him to listen carefully while a tune is hummed. The teacher abruptly stops the song and says, "How many of you know this tune, raise your hands!" The child who raises his hand to identify the music is taken aside and secret police dispatched to his home to arrest and deport his parents to slave labor camps because this particular tune is the signature song of a program message of hope sent over the air waves to Hungary from a free country. Such methods still go on in Hungary, and in other countries under domination of the Communists, where children have been allowed temporarily to live at home until space is made for them in government houses.

A report of the inhuman treatment and lack of respect of woman is contained in documentary evidence submitted to the United Nations by the Hungarian National Council in 1951, concerning a distinguished woman of Hungary, known and beloved by her countrymen:

Deportations aim not only at swift liquidation. The idea is to humiliate victims as much as possible before they succumb to death by privation. One of the most shameful examples is the story of Countess Bethlen. After the First World War, Count Stephen Bethlen, even in the eyes of his enemies, was Hungary's outstanding statesman (he was Prime Minister from 1921 to 1931). Countess Bethlen, a writer, was also descendant of the famous Bethlens of Transylvania. Last summer, she was deported, too. Of her fate, Elet of Innsbruck and Hungaria of Munich wrote: "Though over seventy, she was made to work in the rice fields. When she collapsed, they dressed her in rags and sent her into the fields as a scarecrow. With horror and disgust, well-intentioned natives saw young Communist hoodlums chasing her from field to field. But they could do nothing to help . . ."

Women in America, having their freedom, can stop what the Communists are trying to do in all phases of American life. In Hungary, my family and friends were taken suddenly, by force, and our government was seized by the Communists. Our women had not the opportunity to object. In this country, the attack is not through force but through ideas; ideas particularly directed at the young girls and women of America. With intense fervor, the Communists are trying to inject their philosophy into the arts, especially the theater and literature; educational systems; media of communication; government agencies; politics; and labor unions. Often, their sly methods prove to be very effective. One method depreciates the role of homemaker wherever possible. A certain American high school issued a school folder which encouraged girls to take different classical and specialized courses and at the bottom of the circular was the notation: "We urge our less able girls to study home economics."

41

The Spiritual Woman

It takes alerted women to detect the work of Communist cell members and Communist ideas in their clubs, their parent-teachers associations, their community agencies and educational programs. To those familiar with Communist philosophy, it is easily recognizable even when perhaps unwittingly presented by well-intentioned but uninformed citizens. The party line is often heard in many popular American lecture groups. Not too long ago, an adult school in New York City offered a lecture series on the modern American woman. One of the women lecturers declared:

> The statement, marriage *or* a career, is too broad. We are moving more and more to the idea that mothers and fathers can share parenthood and not homemaking. The mother of the future can have children but she can beget and forget. The time will soon come when we can hire as many homemakers as homes. A full-time qualified homemaker can match woman for mother in every home. To do this, we have to either give the husband enough money to provide adequate help at home, or the community must set up schools, infirmaries, etc., for the care and responsibility of the children.

This is a well-known goal of the Communist regime. Above all else, Communist members work night and day to destroy parental right of authority in the American home. They try to convert all thought and operation to the economic and political goal. Their aim is to put women to work for the economic development of the community, send children to community schools, and establish a system where children will eventually become wards of the government. Under communism, woman is to "beget and forget" her offspring.

What happened in Hungary must not be allowed to happen in America. Women were thrown into camps and bred like animals to meet the demand of the government for more youth to be educated in Communist schools. If some of these women were able to contribute to the economic and intellectual life of the community, between births they were forced into offices, department stores, laboratories, and other government projects. The children thus "begotten and forgotten" by their mothers are the stern, militaristic youths brought up by the government and fanatically loyal to the party line. These are the children who are taught by Communist teachers to destroy religion and its principle of brotherly love. It was Stalin who said, "To maintain and promote the godless movement is a sacred duty of all Soviet citizens, particularly youth." For the past thirty-five years, the Communists have been trying to do away with all religion, Catholic, Jewish, and Protestant. They have used forceful measures in most cases, but sometimes as in America their action is subtle, following the advice of Lenin: "The fight against religion must be conducted with sagacity."

It is important that America's children be taught a belief in God by their mothers with as much vigor as the Communist teachers cast it out of their young. The youth of America may come face to face with the youth of communism either in ideological warfare or in physical combat, and it is with this thought that the words of advice of the greatest Roman orator are recalled: "High priests, you defend the city more securely by religion than by its surrounding walls" (*De Nat. Deorum*, III, 40).

The horrible practice of genocide, one race trying to destroy another, is practiced by the Communists in Soviet Hungary and was described by Edward M. O'Connor of the U.S. Displaced Persons Commission on the 950th anniversary of the crowning of the first King of Hungary:

The civilized world has been shocked again by the most recent atrocities taking place in Hungary under Communist reign. The mass deportations, again underway, demonstrate clearly that a plan has been set in motion to exterminate the Hungarians as a race. Leaders in all walks of life are being arrested in the dead of night and carried off to parts unknown. Their families are left destitute or moved to distant areas of Hungary where there is no housing for them, and where there is little or no chance for them to survive. Just how many thousands have been, and are being, deported to the Artic areas of Siberia is not known as yet. No one is safe from the terror of the Communists

43

—fear is the means used to hold these people in subjugation. The vicious circle that has been established is explained by the Communist government as the "removal of the internal enemy." The internal enemy is, of course, anyone who refuses to adopt the ideologies of communism and who does not cooperate with the regime. If the Communists are to hold power, they must continue this vicious circle because the great masses of the Hungarian people will not adopt the pagan teachings of Moscow. Thus, the present regime in Hungary is proving to the freedom-loving nations of the world that they knowingly and willingly are engaged in the international crime of genocide. With each passing day they are providing ample evidence which one day will confront them as they stand before a Bar of Justice made up of representatives of the Free World.

In Hungary, at the risk of their own lives, women bring food night after night, month after month, to those in hiding from the dreaded secret police. Men, who risk their lives in other ways to help the underground movement, depend upon women to meet the trial of endurance in the heroic bringing of food to hidden ones to keep them alive. There is reported to be a secret army of more than six million men, women, and children within Red Russia borders who are quietly and at great peril united in a spiritual task force. Joseph Johnston tells of this group in *God's Secret Armies Within the Soviet Empire.*[1] Priests, ministers, and rabbis have joined together to strengthen this underground movement. Before he was taken to the dreaded Sopron-Kohida prison, Cardinal Joseph Mindszenty, one of Hungary's leading Catholic prelates, joined Jewish and Protestant brothers to oppose the totalitarian regime in Hungary. Cardinal Mindszenty had long aided the Jewish people and it was generally accepted that during the Nazi invasion, 60 per cent of Budapest's Jews survived the war through his effort.

There are many religious and civic leaders in America who speak out against the Communist philosophy. One well-known religious leader writes:

[1] Joseph Johnston, *God's Secret Armies Within the Soviet Empire,* New York, Putnam, 1954.

Woman and Communism

. . . communism is seen as the dehumanization of man by making him a social animal for whom an economic machine is the total meaning of existence. Christianity agrees with Communists when they point out the need of a revolution, but Christianity places the blame not on institutions, but on men; not on legislation but on legislators, not on politics, but on politicians; not on property but on men. There is absolutely no assurance that when things are commonly produced under communism, man will no longer desire his neighbor's bread card, or his privilege to travel from Russia to free America. Men are not brothers because they divide an apple they have stolen from the garden of the capitalist. But if men are brothers, the apple will be divided without stealing. The early Christians shared their goods because they all possessed the Holy Spirit of Love. Communism tries to establish the impossible; a brotherhood of man without a fatherhood of God.[2]

One of the greatest statesmen of our times, Charles Malik, Minister of Lebanon to the United States, in 1952, stated:

It is the spiritual crisis that is far more disturbing than either the political stresses or the economic strains. In fact, these would never have arisen if the spirit were not in trouble. The rebellious type, the type that knows no respect for anything above itself, the type that delights in destruction and apparently cannot "give God the praise," this type is rampant today. There is a prevailing materialism which is not much superior to the dialectical kind. There is, further, a disturbance of right order. The mind inclines toward the lower, the elemental, the multiform, the dark, the primitive, in place of facing light, truth, being. The only saving grace of this Western materialism is that so far it has not extinguished the great organs of the mind and spirit which still operate in perfect freedom. It is from these agencies that salvation is going to come. What is needed is a great wave of respect and obedience, a fundamental ordering of the welter of desire. More and more men and women of vision are seeing what it is all about, are compassing the challenge in all its dimensions. May their number increase, and may there arise leaders who fear only God and truth, to the end that they speak to the world in ringing words of authority.

[2] Fulton J. Sheen, *Communism and the Conscience of the West*, New York, The Bobbs-Merrill, 1948.

Above all childishness and superficialty, above all softness and self-seeking, grounded in history, disciplined in manner and mind, these leaders should ascetically overcome the essential sensuousness of the age. The greatest challenge is whether the secular and intellectual leadership of the West is adequate to the demands of the moment.

This is a challenge to those of us living in freedom to declare ourselves on the side of God, against anti-God forces, particularly against communism which now threatens the world. Women, with regard for a spiritual goal, must inspire belief in God in their children. I have seen many examples of American women in all walks of life who are alerted to both the subtle and obvious threats of communism. Many are recognizable in each community throughout the nation by their sincere interest and work in civic and social affairs. Youth in America and other unoccupied countries can be trained in the home to emerge in the world as the strong spiritual leaders needed to secure universal freedom.

Communism brought to my family a system under which they were forced to live according to a dictated set of rules. They had to endure the errors of corrupt leaders or be killed. No conscientious person can justify a system which supports the enforced operation of an unholy business known to all men by its identification with brutality, murder, conspiracy, prejudice, and godlessness. All mankind today is aware of these signs as the mark of communism and we are responsible, as trustees of the future, for our choice between religion and the Communist system. I am contemptuous of a political and economic system which promises eventual distribution of material wealth to everyone who may still be alive after murdered brothers and sisters have been disposed of. I believe that under the government of God the rights of free men are guaranteed, woman's place is assured, the dignity of the individual is upheld.

America and the free countries must not be deceived by a Russian foreign policy which offers a false peace. Russian foreign policy can never be trusted until it has denounced communism. Any country sworn to Communist philosophy is pledged to the order of Marx, regardless of what its representatives may say. It is not a question of whether Russian foreign policy may temporarily lean toward America's side in a diplomatic gesture; it is how strong is America's policy on God's side? The spiritual men and women of Hungary and all enslaved countries are joined in a silent prayer that the men and women of free countries will coordinate with spiritual dedication to free the enslaved and restore them in an economic and political system under God which permits freedom of religion and opportunity to accumulate the goods of this world through individual effort without oppression.

V

MILLICENT C. McINTOSH

Woman in Education

WOMEN'S higher education is here to stay. Born in the mid-nineteenth century, through the efforts of pioneer women, it has flourished and spread, until now, one hundred years later, opportunity is open to all girls who wish to embrace it.

During the first half of the last century, education for women was carried on in "female seminaries," many of which later developed into colleges and dropped their preparatory departments. Oberlin College opened its doors to women as well as men in 1833. Elmira, the first women's college in the United States with a program of studies comparable to the men's colleges, was founded in 1855. In rapid succession came others: Vassar in 1865, Wellesley and Smith in 1875, Radcliffe in 1879, Bryn Mawr in 1885, Mt. Holyoke in 1888, and Barnard College in 1889. During this period other colleges were founded in the South, and state universities opened their doors to women; Boston University in 1868 admitted men and women alike, and Cornell University became coeducational in 1872, four years after its opening.

What was a phenomenon only yesterday has become a commonplace today. Thousands of young women are entering our colleges and universities every fall—not bluestockings or feminists, but normal, attractive girls, from families who represent the backbone of many hundreds of communities. It is therefore important to scrutinize the scene; to know the objectives of these students, and to determine what the colleges are doing for our daughters, sisters, professional women, and future wives.

It was inevitable that the first colleges should lay their emphasis on academic standards. Intelligent women, thirsty for knowledge, had long been told that they were incapable of higher learning, and that biologically they were fitted only to produce children. Women's colleges set themselves enthusiastically to the business of proving that these claims were untrue. Stiff entrance requirements were often set up, as difficult as those for the best men's universities. The curriculum of the women's colleges was in most cases patterned on that of their brother institutions. Young women students were deeply serious in their search for knowledge, in their ambition to go on to graduate school or to enter the professions, in their desire to contribute as citizens to making a better world. The men and women who taught in these institutions, along with those who were responsible for their management, were animated alike by loftiness of purpose and by a desire to establish an education which would make great contributions to the women who were brave enough to take advantage of it. All these factors combined to prove beyond a shadow of doubt that women could accept and profit by education on the highest possible plane.

Between 1914 and 1918, the picture began rapidly to change. Formerly, college had been reserved for the girl of exceptional intellect and ambition. During the war, however, the numbers of girls who wished to go to college increased by leaps and bounds. Even parents of wealth and position began to realize that girls must be prepared to take care of themselves, and so sent their daughters to college. Many other girls from substantial families became discontented with a life of leisure, and developed a desire for the opportunities offered by the colleges. As the female undergraduate grew more attractive, she was more sought after by her male counterpart; and girls began to realize not only that college was a good place to prepare to earn one's living, but that it provided a base in which one could have a wonderful time. Applications increased by leaps and bounds; colleges grew and multiplied; state universities took in more and more coeds. During the Second World War, the numbers increased still more because families whose sons were in the army or being educated by the government found that they had spare money with which to educate their daughters.[1]

With the popularization of women's higher education have arisen a number of questions which would never have been asked before 1914. What constitutes the best possible education for large numbers of girls who expect to marry either before or shortly after their graduation from college? [2] Can a curriculum which was well suited to prepare a few women for graduate schools be the best one for the large numbers who now go to college? There is no doubt that recent graduates have been critical of their education as not "preparing them for life." What actually is the answer? Shall the liberal arts colleges for women abandon their traditional routines and emulate the vocational institutions? Shall typing and cooking, interior decorating and home management, baby care and dietetics take the place of fine arts, history, and science? May it be true after all that women should be educated differently from men? The answers

[1] There are now in the United States 154 colleges exclusively for women, including those affiliated with universities, as well as 573 coeducational institutions which admit women. Total number of women enrolled in colleges and universities in 1950 was 720,906, compared with 1,560,392 men enrolled at the same time. Degrees conferred on women in all American colleges in 1950–51 included 105,009 baccalaureates (279,343 to men), 18,901 master's degrees (46,231 to men), and 674 doctorates (6,664 to men).

[2] In a survey (*New York Times Magazine,* June 12, 1949) made of the 784 graduates of the Class of 1934, 82 per cent were married. The percentage of more recent classes is probably higher.

to these questions must be carefully weighed if we are to capitalize on the gains of the past, and go on to a new and more effective future.

I am convinced that the liberal arts curriculum offers intelligent women the best possible preparation for life. Those who today attack the tradition are, in my opinion, criticizing not its fundamental concept, but its applications during the last thirty years. Education can never remain static; it must renew its bases, its applications, its purposes, in terms of the needs of its time. This renewal is what has often been lacking since the First World War. College women have in many cases been given a strictly academic training, with no regard to the lives they will be leading after graduation, with no consideration of the role they will assume as women, with no spiritual quality to give them guidance. So it is that when they relinquish their classrooms for adult routines, they find no answers to their human questions in the textbooks they have studied; they may recall few inspiring examples of good living in the scholars who have instructed them; they confess to feelings of "frustration" as they attempt to take their part in a difficult world, as wives and mothers or as professional or business women.

When we examine the contemporary scene, and attempt to analyze the part women are playing in it, we see the results of their confusion. Many women today are restless and unhappy. Many marriages are unsuccessful, and parent-child relationships are often dislocated. Women have, for the most part, not achieved leadership in good government or social movements. College women graduates have for some reason not usually risen to the top in the professions, in the arts, in national and international affairs. Moral values, in which women have a particular stake, are in a state of flux, and spiritual values have been lost in the general melee. The college graduate, eager to do well her part in the world, finds herself subjected to many strains, which often leave her disillusioned and even bitter.

51

In other words, the world for which our colleges for a hundred years have supposedly been training women as leaders sadly lacks leadership. The good life, toward which allegedly our educational process has been directed, has often not been achieved either personally or communally. The liberal arts tradition has missed fire, not, I am certain, because in itself it lacks depth or permanent values for women, but because we have failed to interpret its concepts realistically, in terms of contemporary human needs.

It is important first of all to understand the part women play in society. Is this part actually different from that of men? Lynn White, President of Mills College, has made a powerful plea [3] that women's education should recognize an "equality of differences as well as equality of identities." I would agree with President White that women as a whole have psychological as well as biological differences from men. If our primary biological role is to produce, nourish, and rear the children in the family, it seems clear that physically and psychologically we have the qualities that nature needs to accomplish that end. On the other hand, there is little evidence to show that these are best developed by any particular *system* of education, or that President White's case for teaching the so-called "minor arts" as part of a college curriculum, and for including the more subtle principles of cookery, holds water as sound educational practice. A report of a college faculty committee, appointed to explore the respects in which college education of women might differ from that of men, seems to state the question clearly:

Men and women differ, but the liberal arts college addresses itself to them as human beings. . . . A curriculum intelligently devised to develop the intellectual, artistic, and social potentialities of the students would, in general, serve men and women equally well. To say

[3] Lynn White, *Educating Our Daughters*, New York, Harper & Brothers, 1950.

this is not to deny that women as women have special problems and that their education may reflect this fact.[4]

So we arrive at the premise that women as human beings need their minds trained, their imaginations cultivated, their perspective enlarged, just as do men. We are still faced, however, with the fact that education in the past seemed to lack some essential in preparing women for life which it is now our task to attempt to analyze. The lack may be summarized in a paraphrase of the above statement: Women as women have special problems and responsibilities, and their education should reflect that fact.

The primary task of all human beings is to understand their own natures and to discover the fullest possible development of the qualities with which they are endowed.[5] The average woman finds her greatest happiness in taking responsibility for the home or for the community, or in establishing a relationship between her work and some constructive end to which it may be directed. In other words, she is primarily concerned with the spiritual and human values.

If this idea be valid, it suggests, first, that liberal arts courses shall, as in the past, cover all fields of knowledge, but that they must be taught with a breadth of understanding which will be considered an essential part of the teaching process. Instruction will relate subject matter to the student's experience, teachers must themselves be sensitive to the needs of our society and of the individuals in our classrooms. Here the special interests and responsibilities of women should be inevitably recognized. History teachers, for example, can present their subject not only as a succession of facts, but also as a revelation of basic truths in human behavior, of basic philosophies which have led to human decadence or progress. Literature, arts, and sciences can be

[4] *Report of Sub-Committee on Women's Education,* Barnard College, New York, 1948, p. 1.

[5] The original material that follows was the basis of a discussion on women's education in *Report of the Dean of Barnard College, 1948–50.*

similarly presented as man's attempts to interpret the world around him, to analyze the beautiful, the true, the good; or to explain the forces that lie behind the universe. The social sciences, the field in which all women eventually participate as wives and citizens, can provide not only the theory but the practice of social behavior and experience.

Moreover, in all branches of learning, women's institutions must emphasize special fields which represent the interests of women. Without changing the character of the liberal arts curriculum, without offering for the bachelor's degree subject matter which, in my opinion, should be imparted in the home or in a trade or vocational school, we could greatly expand the scope of college courses that deal with the contemporary world, with personal relations, and with child study. Colleges should establish better openings for field work, more workshops in the problems of the community, the family, and the government. The natural interest of women in using their leisure to enjoy the arts, if possible as participants but if not as intelligent spectators, should be fully recognized.

Finally, the study of philosophy and religion is of primary importance for a woman. Whether she recognizes it or not, the woman is important in setting the moral and spiritual tone of her family, or of the community in which she lives. She is responsible for training her own children, or in many cases the children of other people. She must be aware of what others have thought and said about the meaning and purposes of life. For it is preeminently the task of women to establish and protect standards, to sustain and inspire men whose immediate responsibility is to provide support and protection for their families.

The right kind of teaching and the imaginative development of the liberal arts curriculum will result in fulfilling the final responsibility of women's higher education: the cultivation of a true sense of values. This includes not only the recognition of spiritual values which I have mentioned, but the understanding of the part women can play in the political and social spheres. It recognizes as essential a proper appraisal of what will bring women the greatest fulfillment. Only recently have we begun to realize that a college does many girls a disservice if it extols intellectual achievement as the highest end in life, by implication suggesting that to be "only a wife and mother" is an inferior role for women to play. Many answers to questionnaires sent to college graduates reflect a demand for a change in the climate of opinion in our colleges, so that graduates face their lives with a sensible realism and a due recognition of what family life is all about. A girl does not need courses in baby-tending to prepare her for motherhood. But she definitely needs some spiritual orientation to that role, a philosophy which does not belittle the home as a place unworthy of her best, and does not glorify the "job" as important beyond everything else. This orientation should, of course, be caught from parents; but it can also be caught from wise teachers, advisers, and administrators. It can never be directly taught, but the awareness of its importance on the part of a superior faculty will go far toward creating the right atmosphere.

In guiding students toward the professions, the colleges will do well to analyze those fields of work where women can find their greatest fulfillment. Such an analysis is outside the scope of this chapter. A word can be said, however, about the importance of interested women in teaching. Before 1914, most college graduates considered teaching as a superior opportunity—in fact, one of the few really good professional opportunities for a woman. Two world wars have opened up many scientific and technical fields to women, which offer them larger salaries and greater worldly prestige. It is high time that we met this situation by presenting teaching in its true light: as a deeply satisfying lifework, one which provides creative opportunities for intellectual development as well as for the fulfillment of all woman's special emotional gifts and interests. Young people inevitably respond to a challenging and rewarding opportunity.

We have been gravely remiss in allowing teaching to become discredited and in not presenting it to college students in its true light.

The situation of the unmarried woman, who goes into business, research, or one of the professions, deserves thoughtful consideration and frank appraisal. Regardless of the fact that her work may be identical with that of her male colleague, she will, I believe, attain her richest fulfillment by recognizing that she can bring to it the special qualities and interests she possesses as a woman. Or she can, if she is realistic about herself, find in interests outside her work fulfillment for her emotional needs. It is the task of the college to recognize these needs, and to give students some degree of insight as to how they can best be met.

No more important problem exists in our contemporary world than that of giving women as well as men the best possible preparation for life. We are living through an uncomfortable period. Many of our communities are torn by debates on the kind of education we should give our children, on the kind of teachers who should be employed, and on the place of religion in the curriculum. The importance of women's education is magnified when we reflect that it is the women, by and large, who set the pattern and the tone of our community discussions. It is the responsibility of our educated women not to lose their heads in these arguments, and not to forget the main issues at stake. We have to keep our minds clearly fixed on the common core of agreement of all intelligent people of good will. We must work from that and not put ourselves on the extremes so that we are in conflict with the forces of history and so that these forces clash and are never resolved.

We have to think out a strategy of good will which will put into practice the tolerance, the ideals of understanding, the recognition of differences that we all have in our society. We must reconcile these into something that will be so constructive that it will sweep before it the fearful, the frustrated, the disappointed, all of us together, who have our own doubts and confusions and despairs, into one common stream of Americans.

The question of how higher education for women can offer the soundest training and the fullest possible opportunity thus requires the deepest consideration and most careful attention. To men, as fathers and husbands and sons, the discovery of good answers to this question is as important as to women. Let us mobilize all our resources to that end, so that women's education may provide true leadership in our contemporary world.

VI

LILLIAN GISH

Woman in Entertainment

T HE theater began when the first little child put a flower behind his ear and said, "Let's pretend." To try to make real the world of our imagination is instinctive to everyone. The theater has a grave responsibility in the moral and cultural development of a country. It was and can always be a handmaiden to religion. It was used by the Greeks alongside their hospitals as a cure or preventive to ills of the mind and the body. Today, in all its phases—television, radio, motion picture, and the living theater— it exceeds in influence the printed word and exerts a tremendous power over the universe. Destructively used, it could do more damage than any weapon, yet strangely enough people are far more fearful of hydrogen and atomic bombs. Our government recognizes the power of these bombs and guides their use, but entertainment as a far-reaching and penetrating force has yet to be properly recognized.

How did this force come into being—this thing we call "theater"? Let us look at the first theater through the eyes of one of America's great artists, the late Robert Edmond Jones. He said:

Let us imagine ourselves back in the Stone Age, in the days of the Cave Man, and the Mammoth and the Alta Mira frescoes. It is night.

We are all sitting together around the fire, Ook and Pow and Pung and Glup and little Zowie and all the rest of us. Over on that side of the fire, the leaders of the tribe are sitting together—the strong men— the men who can run faster and fight harder and endure longer. They have killed a lion today. We are excited about this thrilling event. We are all talking about it. The lion skin lies close by the fire. Suddenly the leader jumps to his feet. "I killed the lion. I followed him. He sprang at me. I struck him with my spear. He fell down. He lay still," he is telling us. We listen, but all at once an idea comes to his dim brain. "I know a better way to tell you. See? It was like this—let me *show* you." In that instant, drama is born. The leader goes on, "Sit round me in a circle—you and you and you—right here, where I can reach out and touch you all" and so, with one inclusive gesture, he makes a theatre. From this circle of eager listeners to Reinhardt's great Shauspielhaus in Berlin is only a step in time.

In its essence, a theatre is only an arrangement of seats grouped in space that the actor, the leader, can reach out and touch and hold each member of his audience. Architects of later days have learned how to add convenience and comfort to this idea, but that is all— the idea itself never changes. The leader continues, "You—Ook—over there—you stand up and be the lion. Here is the lion's skin, you put it on, and be the lion, and I'll kill you, and we'll show them how it was." Ook gets up, he hangs the skin over his shoulders, he drops on his hands and knees and growls—how terrible he is! Of course, he isn't a real lion, we know that. And yet, in some mysterious way, he is the lion. He isn't like the rest of us any longer. He is Ook, all right, but he is a lion, too, and now these two men, the world's first actors, begin to show us what the hunt was like. They act it for us. The hunter lies in ambush, the lion growls. The hunter poses, the lion leaps. We all join in with yells and howls of excitement and terror. The first community chorus. The spear is thrown, the lion falls, and lies still. The drama is finished. Now Ook takes off the lion's skin and sits beside it and is himself again. Ook will be as long as he lives the man who can be a lion when he wants to. The lion's spirit gets into him, and we shall always look up to him and admire him, and perhaps secretly be a little afraid of him. Ook is an actor. He will always be different from the rest of us—a little apart from us—for he can summon spirits. Many thousands of years have passed since that first moment of inspiration when the theatre sprang into being but we still like to make believe, and when an artist like Duse, or Chaliapin, or Pauline Lord speaks aloud in our midst, a thing that is in the minds of all of us and fuses our various moods into one common mood, we are still lost in wonder before this magical art of the theatre. It is really a kind of magic—this art. In some mysterious way, the old, simple ancestral moods still survive in us and an actor can make them live again for a while. We become children once more. We believe.[1]

Pantomine expressed itself in animal mimicry, in war dances, and in the enactment of sacrificial rites. In India and Egyptian civilizations, pantomime developed artistic forms. The Romans developed it as an art and established schools to teach it in their Empire. They wore masks as a means of distinguishing their characters. This later developed into ballet as we know it. When masks were discarded, it became dumb show in England. Religious mystery plays of the Middle Ages showed traces of the old pantomime. In Italy, it became the *commedia dell'arte*, using popular figures like clowns and others, with song, dance, and jest, to tell their improvised story. In the seventeeth century, the first traces of the motion picture are to be found in the little island of Bali, east of Java. In Germany and England, pantomime became a rude form of dramatic buffoonery. It retarded the drama in Germany until 1737, when pantomime was banished and gave way to the birth of modern extravaganza. By the nineteenth century, it had nearly disappeared.

During this time, religious plays were enacted outside church buildings. Stained glass windows were used as backgrounds and liturgical drama became popular. Later, groups formed to give miracle plays. Some of these detached themselves from ecclesiastical authority and farce was allowed to creep into the theater as these plays were moved to the public squares. The Passion Play, which is an exception, was given at Oberammergau and has continued almost unbroken since 1633; this and *Jeder-*

[1] Robert Edmond Jones, *The Dramatic Imagination*, New York, Duell Sloan and Pearce, 1941.

mann, performed in the public square at Salzburg, give some idea of the impressiveness which these dramas can attain.

I like to divide the theater with which we are familiar today into three parts—the Greek classic, the Shakespearean era, and the modern Ibsenesque drama. Where do we find woman? We find that only a few women enjoyed a cultural position in the Greek concept. They were not allowed to take part on the stage although some were able to support the theater as patronesses and spectators. Listen to Aristotle in his *Poetica,* when writing of the good in character, and know the status of woman at that time. He said, "Such goodness is possible in every type of character, even in a woman or a slave, though the one is perhaps an inferior and the other a worthless human being."

In the Shakespearean period, the attitude toward women in general had improved since the days of Aristotle. Woman was more widely recognized and she was accepted as a spiritual force in society, although she still suffered abuses of her position. Themes of plays ran from great tenderness to the most rugged soul-searching of plots. On stage, men played the roles of women because it was socially taboo for a lady to appear. This attitude continued until William Congreve, in the late seventeenth century, engaged women to play in *Love for Love.* Thus began the emergence of woman as a real force in the theater and she was finally allowed to fill feminine roles. Mrs. Bracegirdle and Nell Gwynne are perhaps the best known to us of this period. Nell Gwynne attracted the eye and won the heart of a king which must have aroused considerable excitement in women coming into the theater.

Shakespeare's era placed acting on a professional level. Charges for admission were introduced primarily to meet actors' salaries and strolling troubadours were then able to settle down and devote full time to acting. Because moderation prevailed in the profit motive, a high cultural level was possible. Prose, poetry, and playwriting were pursued by gentlemen of the court and universities, as well as by professionals. Playwrights acknowledged woman's moral influence in society and created roles for her which brought about social reform. When Ibsen wanted to show that the individual was more important than society, or the state, he used a woman, Nora, in *The Doll's House*, to prove his point. Ibsen changed the drama of the world. During the century since he wrote his first play, the imitators of this great playwright and mystic have been legion. While he had no allegiance to any religious body, he always wrote for an intenser Christianity.

Where do women come into this theater scene in America? Let us start with Harriet Beecher Stowe whose work, *Uncle Tom's Cabin,* was of such social significance that Abraham Lincoln said it was mainly responsible for our Civil War. A century later, all Americans are familiar with this story, and Topsy and Eva have almost become a part of our common language. A part of this story was danced in the popular musical, *The King and I,* starring the late Gertrude Lawrence. Each country is primarily interested in its own history and this is one reason why *The King and I* enjoyed success.

We have had many outstanding women as playwrights in the American theater. Our first legitimate play, *The Contrast,* by Royall Tyler, was produced in New York City in 1789. Forty years later, a great-granddaughter of Francis Lewis, signer of the Declaration of Independence, translated and produced Voltaire's *Alzire* when she was only fourteen years old. She shocked her friends by giving public readings in her early twenties as Mrs. Mowatt and, soon after, wrote her most successful play, *Fashion.* She then began an extended career, acting in this country and in England. When she retired in 1854, Mr. Lloyd Morris tells us in his fine book, *Curtain Time,* "She had done what nobody believed possible, entered a profession condemned by Puritans, burdened by the imputation of loose morals, and triumphantly demonstrated that a lady could rise to greatness in it without ceasing to be a lady."

Fanny Kemble of the famous English acting family had

enormous success in our theater. She married a "rich" American and went to live on his plantation in Georgia with her two daughters. Later she wrote and published in 1863 *A Residence on a Georgia Plantation*, which was one of the influences that caused the British to cease helping the Confederacy. After her divorce, Mrs. Kemble returned as a matronly figure to the theater and gave readings that inspired Herman Melville and Emerson. Longfellow dedicated a sonnet to her and Hawthorne put her in the *Blithedale Romance*. But she would never play in the South because she did not want her salary of two or three thousand dollars a week to be paid by slave-earned money. At about the same time, Laura Keene was proving that she could manage her own theater and company as well as act. It was to see her play, *The Country Cousin,* on that fatal Good Friday night that Abraham Lincoln came to her theater. She was said to have held his head in her lap after the tragic shooting. During her last year, a child entered her company billed as Minnie Maddern, who later added the name of Fiske. By 1879, young John Drew was acting with that veteran of nineteen years, the talented comedienne, Ada Rehan. By 1883, American vaudeville had originated in Boston, when Benjamin F. Keith opened a small museum and show in a vacant candy store next to the old Adams House in Washington Street. The motion picture reached us in much the same way about twenty-five years later, after it emerged from Mr. Edison's laboratory in 1894.

During these early years of the theater, actors with few exceptions were set apart from "genteel" society. In many cases they had earned their bad reputation and society was justified in chastising them. They wandered over the land like vagabonds, often stranded without money in faraway places and forced to get back to base as best they could. Helen Hayes tells about touring as a child with John Drew, when only he would be accepted by first-class hotels but not the other actors. When I went to Ohio to visit my aunt in the summers of my childhood, I was

warned not to mention that I was on the stage because children
would not be allowed to play with me.

Actors and actresses today are accepted as members of a
respected profession and for what we are individually. Since
most of us in the theater live without benefit of press agents,
what we are is easily discernible. Actresses whose cinema names
are household words throughout the nation and the world have
a tremendous responsibility to society. Those of good conscience
continue to assert a proper influence for moral integrity by
setting a good example of conduct in both their public and
private life.

With the advent of motion pictures came a force for good or
evil far more potent than the written word. D. W. Griffith, the
father of the formula for telling a story with a camera, told us
that we were taking the first baby steps in a new medium that
had been predicted in the Bible. He said the universal language
had been found and, if used properly, it could bring about the
millennium. The silent films at their best had the resources of
universality. Pictures bring to the child his early understanding
of the world about him. Love, hate, desolation, despair, joy,
ecstasy, defeat, triumph, these are universal emotions; conveyed
by words they offer difficulties to remote peoples, but conveyed
by movement of face and body they are immediately recognizable. A laugh or a sob is the same the world over. A simple waltz
by Johann Strauss may remain alien to a Chinese ear, just as
Chinese music may sound strange to us! A drama by Ibsen may
be completely unintelligible in translation to many Hindus! But
the pantomime of a Chaplin can make the Hindus and Chinese
laugh as understandably as we. Pantomime as the aboriginal
means of communication had its greatest outlet in the silent
movie.

The American film industry led the world in its production
and world-wide distribution of these movies. With the advent of
the "talkie," it lost its universal leadership. Foreign language
countries set up their own studios and produced their own

language films. D. W. Griffith foresaw this when he made the first talking picture in 1921 called *Dream Street*. After this production, he discontinued the use of words which he felt were a barrier to being understood by the rest of the world. He used music instead which he believed would better serve universal understanding. However, the talking picture gained tremendous popularity in this country and developed into a powerful device to catch the attention of the public. In 1917, Lloyd George, Prime Minister of England, sent for David W. Griffith and asked him to go to work for the British and French governments. "We want you to persuade the American people to go to war for us. Since you have the greatest machine for propaganda the world has ever seen, this will not be difficult," he said.

A few years ago, we were to be allowed to send a group of films into a land behind the Iron Curtain. Whether these films were sent, I have never been able to find out. But had we sent ten fine pictures concerned with our way of life, they could have persuaded more people than a hundred ambassadors. We should have films telling what America is today and how we developed our way of life and our form of government. Where are the films about George Washington, Thomas Jefferson, Benjamin Franklin, Thomas Paine, James Madison, and other forefathers of our country? And the thrilling early record of our initial struggle? We have had the biography of the gangster, Dillinger; the story of the trombone player, Glenn Miller; two films about Al Jolson, and not one about the father of the motion picture industry, D. W. Griffith! Is there any wonder that the picture theaters are closing throughout our land? The more than two-year run of Cinerama in New York City proves that there is no lack of interest in films. It does prove that this medium, generally speaking, has failed to bring the type of entertainment that is of cultural and educational value. There has been too much glamorizing of that which is fundamentally wrong. As one eminent leader recently said when addressing a motion picture industry group, "Glamorizing evil over virtue never succeeds. All the whims of human nature may find rightful expression in the drama but if the wrong is represented as right, we are bound to destruction eventually. It is the same when individuals of evil repute are glamorized and lifted to the level of virtue."

The motion picture is the common story book, newspaper, and textbook of the twentieth century. It deals for the most part with primitive instincts and impulses, human peace and alarm, happiness and ache, ambition and dream. What concept of the American woman does the motion picture depict? While Madame Pandit was President of the Eighth Session of the General Assembly of the United Nations, she said on the radio that "the Hindu women were fearful of becoming like the American women." The Hindu woman's idea of the American woman has come to her through our films which, Madame Pandit said, "were the greatest enemy America has." Some time after Madame Pandit's radio comment, I read a press release in the American newspapers in July 1954 that confirmed her remarks. As reported from New Delhi, India, about thirteen thousand housewives and mothers in Delhi demanded action to "control the evil of the cinema," in a memorandum submitted to Prime Minister Jawaharlal Nehru. The women leaders criticized modern movies as a "major menace to the moral health of children" and pressed for legislation to curb the evil.

The effect on our world neighbors of these portrayals of the American woman is appalling. Too often she is depicted as a bored housewife, an overly ambitious shrew, a gangster's girl friend, all interested primarily in money and sex. This is the conclusion that many of our non-American friends and enemies come to, and they can scarcely be blamed for this idea. In this country, the justification and defense for these caricatures of the American woman by those responsible is always the threadbare cliché, "we give the public what it wants." That laconic answer reveals an undiscriminating audience but it still does not excuse those who control the medium for their lack of responsibility for the formation of national ideals.

Woman in Entertainment

It is in the twentieth century that woman's real opportunity for influence in the entertainment field has come about and I am sorry to find that we are strangely unconscious of it. These are strong words but I shall try to prove them true because of the seriousness of the situation. Theater consists of three groups: first, the man or woman who writes the play or story; secondly, the group that brings it to life on the stage, screen, or microphone; and thirdly, the audience who looks and listens. All three are equally important. No, the last is the most important. When three fourths of our audiences are women, then it is the women who are most responsible for the state of entertainment in this country today. Since woman has a responsible interest in the kind of portrayal made of her, one finds it difficult to believe that she can really be satisfied with what is represented of her. A Carrie Nation is not the type needed for a transformation in the field of entertainment. We do not seek destruction but an elevation to mature morality. This is not a plea for censorship because censorship is not the answer to a lack of responsibility; only an education to a sense of keen responsibility is the real answer. Neither do we declare a judgment of condemnation. On the contrary, much of the work accomplished in these media is praiseworthy. But woman must insist upon a more genuine and dignified portrayal of herself for national and international audiences.

Television is one of the newer and most powerful machines invented for entertainment and it is capable of destroying the essence of culture and education when it is misused. It is influential because it comes right into your home and because it is a kind of X-ray machine on the human psyche. If you look closely, you can tell the nature of those you watch, regardless of the words they use. Radio can fool you, but not television—unless you are the fool.

Our neighbor Canada has its minister of fine arts; the French Government has looked after its Comédie Française since it was founded in 1680; the British Government is a patron of the arts.

The increasing interest taken by Parliament in making Britain's cultural heritage better known and more within the reach of all is expressed through the Arts Council, the British Film Institute, and the British Council. In 1950–51, the government expenditure on promotion of the arts, including the British Broadcasting Corporation, was $81,998,000. Sweden, with only fourteen million population, has a State Theater in Stockholm, Gothenburg, and Malmö. These excel in facilities for staging anything this country has ever known, including Radio City Music Hall. They have not only sent us many talented players, trained in their Royal Dramatic Theater in Stockholm, but their immortal August Strindberg was the inspiration for our own Eugene O'Neill. The Swedish people have a fine living theater, which permits everyone who wishes to see all the great drama of the past and present. Significantly, their crime rate is among the lowest in the world.

With the great influence on society of these media—motion picture, radio, television, and the legitimate stage, all under the heading of entertainment for aesthetic purposes, our nation should have a secretary of fine arts in the President's Cabinet. This would give dignity and importance to the theater which should be considered as one of the fine arts. Actually, the government already makes use of all these theater channels to reach the public and it is time that it officially recognizes theater as a means of cultural and educational development.

We need a national theater like other cultured lands. In a democracy we do not want government domination over any field but we do need government assistance which would help provide conditions under which theater art would flourish. We do not propose that government invade the realm of private initiative and investment but, rather, that it become a patron of the arts. The creative abilities of individuals must be kept free of government control. But with government assistance, even if it is only by recognition through a national tribute to a fine play, script, telecast or film, it would at least establish a goal for which all could strive.

We have strong spiritual and cultural leadership in our President under the Constitution. When the President realizes the important contribution the media of theater make to our lives, then the theatre will receive the dignity, recognition, and help it has long needed.[2]

Women, representing three fourths of audiences, have the challenge to educate all media of entertainment to a sense of moral responsibility. This challenge confronts not only members of audiences but the women who are employed in these media. The power of woman in America today is second to no other. They and they alone must take the initiative in maintaining good theater. It is up to them. This is their field since they are mainly responsible for training the generations of the future. They know how strongly youth can be influenced by all branches of the theater. America needs a vibrant theater.

[2] Miss Gish, with a pre-publication copy of her chapter, and with the approval of the Editor, made a special trip to Washington, D. C. to plead personally with the President for this recognition. Miss Gish met with the President and the First Lady and the success of her mission is reflected in this part of the President's State of the Union Message, January 6, 1955:
"In the advancement of the various activities which will make our civilization endure and flourish, the federal government should do more to give official recognition to the importance of the arts and other cultural activities. I shall recommend the establishment of a federal advisory commission on the arts within the Department of Health, Education and Welfare, to advise the federal government on ways to encourage artistic endeavor and appreciation. I shall also propose that awards of merit be established whereby we can honor our fellow citizens who make great contribution to the advancement of our civilization."

VII

PATRICIA C. CROWLEY

Woman and Family Life

TODAY in many American homes there seems to be a complete reversal in the traditional family life; the woman is the authoritative head of the house; no longer is it the man. The children look to her for guidance in all matters and rarely to the father who often furnishes only the funds to the family group, in an irritable, preoccupied, or quasi-comic manner. Perhaps this is because his work is a matter of tedious routine which removes from him any sense of individual accomplishment. The lack of opportunity for initiative and creativeness can result in a job dissatisfaction which builds up frustrations and hostilities felt in the home. With a work background of regimentation, a man can return home unprepared for leadership and ill at ease in his rightful position of authority. The woman takes over in many cases not because she wants to, but because she has to. When this occurs, a deep scar is inflicted upon her feminine psychology. She develops an unwomanly aggressiveness and dominance that lead to a long chain of conflicts between herself and her husband. She can lose the personal dignity and security that belong to her as a woman and resort to an unnatural competition with her husband.

The modern husband will find more stability and happiness in his home life if he regains his proper place as head of his family and gives recognition by his thinking and acting to his wife's true womanly attributes, helping her to develop them by a notable fulfillment of his own masculine role. The intelligent woman realizes that unless her husband develops his masculinity and takes an authoritative place in society, he does not reach his full stature as a man, and both home and nation suffer from his weakness. Man exposed to the limitations and obstacles of a materialistic philosophy outside the home can easily lose confidence in himself. His wife has the responsibility not only to him but to the nation to reestablish this confidence by acknowledging him as the head of his family and giving him the respect due to this position. She can defer to his judgment, help him make decisions, seek his advice, recognize his efforts, and, above all, understand his role in society. To do this, she must first convince herself of the justification for man to be invested with authority. She must review the reasons for this claim by a more penetrating consideration of the structure of the family and its spiritual values.

The family has been considered a sacred and indispensable unit of society for centuries. People who believe in God have always looked upon it as a divine institution. For those who believe in the redemption it has been a sacramental institution as well. To trifle with marriage vows or marriage rights was once considered a betrayal of the sacred institutions of God. Those with vision have urged the world to protect and foster the virtuous family, to honor and enhance the sacredness of marriage with religious rite. But today many people disregard or deny affiliation with any religious faith. For them, church weddings in modern society are thought to be merely superstitious remnants of what was once a thoroughly religious ceremony in Western society. Civil law has entered more and more into domestic relations and has omitted from the marriage contract its sacred character and its dependence upon a creating God.

The primary objective of marriage for some has become the selfish pleasure and satisfaction to be derived by the contracting parties. If the husband is no longer regarded as the legitimate head of domestic society, enjoying authority from God and burdened with responsibility to God for the benefit of society, there is no particular reason why the word "obey" should be part of the woman's relationship. The misinterpretation of "equality" has brought about the notion that the religious idea of obedience is a relic of the old feudalistic domination by the male. According to this theory, there is no center of authority in domestic society. It is considered unworthy of woman to defer to her husband's decision. Perhaps this is why disrespect for parental authority has grown in modern life.

The current idea of marriage is what a man and a woman by their own decision want to make out of it. So many people feel that they must not be bound by old religious laws which to the "free" mind of modern man make marriage a burdensome state. These men and women want no responsibilities and what they do with marriage they believe is their own concern. For these, the state of marriage depends entirely upon their convenience and their desires, not upon any plan of God. In other words, no laws of God or of nature are allowed to interfere with man's convenience. Marriage set up in this climate is a negation of its traditional meaning. Perhaps some may think this new attitude is progress in freedom. To others it is more like retrogression, unless the whole tradition of Western society for centuries is to be lightly dismissed as a fraud.

Laws made by men can be changed, abrogated, or circumvented by men. We know that the civil status of marriage grows weaker and weaker. Many men and women seem to have more regard for business contracts than they have for marriage contracts. Moral cowardice is nowhere more manifest in America than in our divorce mills. From newspaper accounts we read that many of these divorcing parties do not hesitate to lie and perjure themselves when they set about to break the civil contract. When marriage is made to depend exclusively on the convenience and pleasure of man and woman, and not on a solemn contract before God with uncompromising obligations, the marriage bond is only as lasting as the pleasure and convenience of the contracting parties.

Within a century America has shown a 600-per-cent increase in divorce and the approved reasons in some cases have made us the laughingstock of the world. Evidently some couples think it is a better world if we can get rid of everything we do not like. Such people, many of whom are proclaimed as celebrities, have become selfish, sense-dominated children who go into tantrums of divorce and adultery when they cannot have their own way. They do not recognize any authority higher than earthly man, no obligation except to man, no responsibility except to man's pleasure, no acknowledgment of the law of God. The instability of modern man is nowhere more evident than in domestic society.

A nation with a divorce mentality is likely to become an irresponsible nation, guided more by expediency and temporal advantage than by moral law. If people mock life's most fundamental relationship, the family unit, they will eventually mock every other relationship, including the relationship of citizen to government and government to citizen, forgetting that this country was founded upon trust in God and upon observance of the moral law. It is chimerical to think that people who have no sense of responsibility in domestic society can maintain a sense of responsibility in civil society for any length of time. If we do not protect marriage and the family from the decay induced by a violation of the principles upon which this nation was founded, how can we expect to protect civil society from the decay which must follow the violation of these principles? The national moral cowardice, selfishness, and irresponsibility proved by the widespread divorce rate are the handwriting on the wall of our national life. Women of all faiths who recognize the significance of it will unite in protest against the obstacles which threaten the foundations of their homes.

We know the sad effect which divorce has upon the children. How can we expect decency and restraint of a youth which is constantly confronted with the promiscuity and adultery of its

73

elders? Whether we like it or not, our young people are a living testimony to our parents and our society. Absence of the authority which should be vested in the father as his moral right is the background of so many American children that it has cast upon society a group of independent, selfish young people. Our youth resents discipline, supervision, and correction, because it has not been given a sense of right and wrong nor of responsibility before God and man for action. Our youth has not absorbed a sense of justice because their whims have been catered to by well-meaning but injudicious parents. Parental authority based on moral principles and discipline in its highest meaning should be restored to family life. Discipline does not mean physical abuse, nor display of unjustified temper; it does mean firm insistence upon recognition of right and wrong, and insistence upon unequivocal respect for authority. In some cases children are trained for freedom, not for virtue. The day is past when we can blame illiteracy for delinquency. The homes of our delinquents are not at all exclusively the homes of the underprivileged. Youth crimes have climbed the rungs of the social ladder. J. Edgar Hoover, head of the Federal Bureau of Investigation, believes that the cause for the growing crime wave among the young is defective home life and a lack of religious training.

Those of us who are mothers have seen the growing tendency among many of our friends to shift the total responsibility for the education of the child to the school. As one of our leading educators has commented, "Too often the home is a centrifugal force in society instead of being the magnetic center of spiritual and cultural living." Gradually the school becomes the substitute for the home, and teachers become substitutes for parents.

The growing lack of responsibility among children is a critical problem. Some families fail to develop a sense of responsibility. Satisfaction of individual desires, both of parents and of children, is overemphasized. The common good is little stressed or exemplified. Group participation and mutual aid and consideration are as healthy in the family as in any other society. We speak

74

nostalgically about the farming family, where the members as a group worked, played, and prayed together and were well adjusted to society. Surveys today suggest that many dismissals in industry are due to social incompetence. This helps to illustrate that the home as the training ground is failing to turn out well-adjusted citizens.

Children need a sense of security, of belonging; a feeling that they are capable of great achievement. They should feel that their contribution to the life of the family is worth something. To achieve this sense of belonging and contribution to the group, some parents hold family discussions where the children have a chance to express their views about the order and discipline of the home. Family discussions present an excellent opportunity to convey the notion of the common good. These family discussions can begin on the spur of the moment, but the father and mother must prepare the agenda. Such gatherings help to promote a sort of self-government within the family, with the father as head. A certain amount of trial and error, with a minimum of iron-clad rules, helps a child to develop a sense of responsibility. The child should be given final decision on some things which have been delegated to his responsibility. In the spending of a birthday dollar, for instance, the child may seek parental advice, but care should be taken to see that the final decision as to what he will spend it for rests with him. After a while, he will come to see that his judgment was, or was not, sound. In making his choice for better or for worse, he is strengthening his sense of responsibility. The practical mind of woman can determine the hour and the frequency of these meetings and their regularity. The father should always preside. Children who have a share in the family responsibility will do their part in discharging their duties and will make the life of the group more pleasant.

We have found that family meetings can be a fascinating experience. Parents are pleased and surprised that children are capable of prescribing discipline and are more disposed to accept punishment which they have helped to define. The meetings, lasting only a few minutes, can be held after dinner or during some other occasion when the family is together. Each child should be called upon to participate happily. These meetings should never be allowed to become menacing or fearful. The name of God, an education to His commandments, to loving Him and obeying His commandments, should come up frequently in this and in other family conversations in the homes of all families who believe in God, of whatever denomination.

Many forces are being brought to bear on married women to return to work even while their children are still young enough to need a mother's care. Today more than ten million married women work. In other words, one out of every four married women works outside the home. The need to work is understandable for married women who must provide necessities for the family, because of a husband's illness, widowhood, or other justified reasons. Substitute teaching in public schools, or teaching in private schools, where shorter hours can be arranged and adapted to the individual family needs, is possible. In many cases it is desirable for married women whose children are grown to return to work. But we question the reasoning of a woman who turns her small child over to a stranger while she goes out to earn money solely to maintain a relatively high standard of living. For the women who thoughtlessly say that some women are just not capable mothers, that the child is better off with someone whose maternal instincts are more developed, this is a denial of their fundamental womanhood. It is an admission of their failures as women. To those who say that the child is better off with material benefits, in excess of reasonable necessities, which could be bought from the salary of the working mother, we say that a child's happiness is not entirely dependent upon or determined by the amount of material possessions of working parents. A mother of young children may, by going to work, help to buy a new house. But what does it profit her children if the walls of a brand-new house do not encompass the assuring

presence of their own flesh and blood mother? It is unanimously
agreed by all working mothers that the baby sitters left in the
house are not proving "quite satisfactory." Instead of reaping the
true happiness experienced by fulfilling with love the responsibility of motherhood, many modern women trudge to daily work,
leaving behind a new house, a new car, new furniture, new
appliances, new gadgets. They buy new coats, new clothes, new
hats necessary to keep their jobs; they spend lunch money with
co-workers, and return home tired but triumphant—to survey
their material possessions. Their love for inanimate objects makes
it all worth while. Their love for animate human beings—their
children—suffers atrophy for want of exercise. No one denies the
advantages of enhanced living conditions; a man's reasonable
ambition can most worthily be directed toward earning these
things for his wife and family. But never will they bring happiness to him or to his family if acquired by separating the mother
from the child, by trading the responsibility of child-rearing for
a new house, by substituting a paid worker for the natural
companionship of a true mother, or by focusing on the playthings
of materialism as the foundation of home life.

The increase in divorces, broken homes, and juvenile delinquency runs parallel to the increase in working mothers. It is
the restless, undisciplined age we live in that drives so many
young married couples to want their material desires to be ful-
filled at once. Parents may have given years of sacrifice and
hard labor in industry, in business, and in the home to accumulate the money which, in their more mature years, they use to
raise their standard of living, send their children to college, buy
necessary clothes, and enjoy general social and educational
advancement. The young married woman, in having accepted
these hard-earned gifts, must not expect immediately the same
standard of living it took her parents years to attain. In haste to
maintain these social advantages or to further them, she should
not lose sight of the element of justice inherent in having to earn
what we get—a principle upon which the strength and durability

of our forefathers thrived. The real purpose of marriage, its spiritual foundation, should not be set aside in the scramble to accumulate material possessions. Mrs. Walter Ferguson, well-known columnist, says:

What spiritual aims do we pursue? These, I think, are the questions before us. Women have made tremendous progress in thirty years—as citizens, as wage earners, as individuals who, like men, gained the right to work out their own destiny. Yet during that period, American marriage and family life have suffered tragic reverses. The worship of the gadget has become such an obsession that millions of mothers are forced to leave their homes and children to supplement the family income. What will it profit us to rearrange the affairs of the globe if at the same time we create an economy that destroys the American home?

The thinking of some women that household work is dull is not accepted by intelligent and practical women. Many wise women are finding much satisfaction in releasing their energies and creativeness in the skill of domestic crafts. They realize that any boredom or lack of satisfaction from working in the home will evidence itself in mounting nervous tensions finally bursting upon husbands and children in strident voice and angry action. If a woman in business finds the routine of work boring, at either an intellectual or physical level—as she often does—she must adjust to the situation or be fired. No one wants a killjoy in the office or in the factory and her adjustment to the situation is helpful to herself as well as to others around her. Perhaps because there is a lack of authority in the home, many women feel free to indulge their bad dispositions. Housekeeping requires exact attention and is truly an art. This was mentioned by Miss Sarah Gibson Blanding, President of Vassar College, at a meeting held at the Randolph-Macon Woman's College Conference on Liberal Education in the Contemporary World, as reported by the New York *Herald Tribune.*

A college education is highly valuable to a girl who intends to get married and rear a family. This is true because the problems that confront modern wives try the intellect, as well as the soul. The contemporary world demands that the homemaker understand such matters as tax forms, traffic violations, draft notices and school laws and truancy, and have a working knowledge of NATO, Iranian oil, Congressional investigations and the atom-bomb. In case anyone should think the housewife with the liberal education has shunned the kitchen arts in her quest for wider knowledge, Miss Blanding pointed out that a Vassar graduate won a $25,000 first prize in a national baking contest. This superior cake baker also had had more than a passing knowledge of Congressional investigations, Iranian oil and the like. "The liberal arts college graduate," Miss Blanding said, "will be a good homemaker if she is interested in human beings, which is something that college has done much to develop in her." Miss Blanding also said that the old bromide about college women not marrying in numbers equal to non-college women doesn't hold good. Statistics show that a slightly larger percentage of college women now marry than do the non-college girls, she added. They marry young too.

The modern wife must act as business manager, retail buyer, electrician, handyman, and chef. Sometimes no matter how hard she tries and works at all these jobs, she fails to find the work rewarding and is unhappy. One of the reasons for this is not knowing which role to develop over the other. Mrs. Samuel Abbott Smith, in an unpublished study called "Household Engineering" says, "There is a scheme of values in every housewife's work, whether she knows it or not, and this scheme affects for good or ill the health, the tastes, the character of those for whom she cares and those with whom she associates."

Some women understandably drift into an unhappy pattern of marriage and become so used to its general tone of discouragement that they fail to arouse themselves to correct the situation. Their living lacks quality and their marriage lacks fiber. The natural instigator to restore and preserve a healthy family life is the woman, who arouses herself from discouragement and apathetic resignation and uses the courage, firmness, and tact of her womanhood to start a rehabilitation of the family for the harmony so necessary to it and to the general tone of the neighborhood. The individual family cannot be really happy if it concerns itself only with its own members. The family does not live in isolation. It lives in a neighborhood, which in turn is part of a series of communities all the way up to the world community. How can we expect peace in the community of nations if we often fail so miserably to bring a spirit of peace, friendliness, and love into our neighborhood?

Woman, as a good neighbor, must be willing to help others. She ought to radiate a welcoming charity so that her home may be a center of attraction and not a moated castle. The job of integration falls most heavily upon the wife, but the children must be taught to share in the work of the home and the good-neighbor policy, too. Children can learn from the hospitality of the home that it is possible to live a full spiritual life even in these days. Fathers and mothers can show their love of God through their love of neighbor. They will learn that it is possible to feed the hungry, to give drink to the thirsty, to clothe the naked, to give shelter to the homeless. All people have deep capacities for love and service that need to be activated and cultivated. Since woman's primacy is love, it is for her to create the bond of unity in the family. If love is to be the atmosphere of the home, then it seems that woman must reveal the goodness in herself and discover and emphasize the goodness in her husband and children. Love is evoked only by the vision of goodness. Exclusive attention to defect and failure destroys the bond of love.

Husbands and wives are fitted by their life experience to help remove the social pressures which make family life difficult. Each couple should spread its domestic teamwork beyond the home. Many families of different religious denominations are awakening to the need of their own group effort to promote general peace and harmony in the community. One such organization of couples doing this is the Christian Family Movement. In

CFM thousands of couples are meeting together every two weeks in small neighborhood groups throughout the country. They make good use of the complementary natures of husbands and wives. They know that families are influenced by the environment in which they live. They know that the present materialistic environment is often at war with spiritual ideals. Confronted by this hostility between the real and the ideal, and realizing that only a united group effort can effect a change, they have banded together to observe the state of affairs in their neighborhood, to judge the facts, and then to act in a small, practical way to change the situation. CFM sees its approach as a manageable method for family and neighborhood unity which is a necessary prerequisite for world unity.

What is the ideal wife like? The Old Testament gives us valuable clues in this quotation: [1]

A man who has won a vigorous wife has found a rare treasure, brought from distant shores. Bound to her in loving confidence, such a man will have no need for spoils. Content, not sorrow, she will bring him as long as life lasts. . . . Ripe wisdom governs her speech, but it is kindly instruction she gives. She keeps watch over all that goes on in her house, not content to go through life eating and sleeping. That is why her children are the first to call her blessed, her husband is loud in her praise. Unrivalled art thou among all the women that have enriched their homes. Vain are the winning ways, beauty is a snare; it is the woman who fears the Lord that will achieve renown. Work such as hers claims its reward; let her life be spoken of with praise at the city gates. . . .

In modern society, the mentally frail woman has been so idealized that a common phrase among men is, "I won't tell my wife about this crisis; I don't want to upset her." But the vigorous woman of today will want to share the hopes and fears, the joys and sorrows. If right order is established in the home, it will become again the fundamental unit of society. And out of this

[1] The Book of Proverbs, 31:10, An Alphabet of Good Housewifery.

sharpening and cleaning up of family life will come a clear moral tone to guide the family and the nation.

Elizabeth Goudge describes this fact so well in *Pilgrim's Inn*: [2]

> . . . it was homemaking that mattered. Every home was a brick in the great wall of decent living that men erected over and over again as a bulwark against the perpetual flooding in of evil. But woman made the bricks and the durableness of each civilization depended upon their quality.

The unity and strength of the nation depend upon the quality and endurance of its individual family members. Women with vision, women of all faiths, must unite to make the true quality of family life endure, to give children moral codes to live by and to stem the irreligious tides that threaten the walls of our homes.

[2] Elizabeth Goudge, *Pilgrim's Inn*, New York, Coward McCann, 1948.

VIII

HON. MARY T. NORTON

Woman in Industry

IN THE early days of my Congressional experience as Chairman of the District of Columbia Committee, one Congressman would always say, when I submitted a bill for the District, "I yield to the lady." This finally goaded me into answering him, "You are yielding to a member of Congress who is elected just as you are."

For a woman to hold office in state and national governmental bodies is no longer a novelty, and men have become so accustomed to working with women in public affairs that such an attitude as that displayed by my colleague back in 1932 would now seem absurd.

In industry, women have come to be accepted as rightfully belonging to the nation's labor force and able to hold many responsible positions which were formerly thought of as "men's jobs." The general attitude toward working women, and the attitude of women themselves toward their work, has changed considerably in my lifetime.

I recall that at the turn of the century not many women were accepted as good risks in responsible positions. My own experience is a typical example of the thinking of many men at that time. I was sent to fill a secretarial position at 17 Battery Place,

New York. When the president of the corporation saw me he was a bit rude—"But I don't want a woman to upset my business," said he. I assured him I was harmless and would try to do as little damage as possible. I remained there for six years.

Another condition frequently found at the time of my youth, and one hard to understand today, was the feeling of social inferiority experienced by some girls when they entered the labor market. It was common for a girl who held a job in business or industry to remark that she was "working for pin-money." Of course, this was not true. Then, as now, women worked mainly because of economic necessity. But the remark about pin-money seemed to give some degree of superiority in the mind of the woman worker.

Today, women are proud of the positions they hold in business, industry, in the professions, in politics. The women themselves, as well as the men with whom they work, have come to realize that they are capable of giving and willing to give as reliable service as men. In this day and age, the functioning of our nation's economic and social life—our modern civilization—is dependent upon the work of women and men.

The mothers of the world have always been the molders of character and the reliable workers at all trades in the home. Mother must be a tactful counselor and friend when disputes arise; and when through death or economic necessity she must provide for her family, she must prepare herself for a job. It is well therefore to give thought to how women can work best in industry for themselves and their families when it becomes necessary to do so. Since war changes the lives of many women whose husbands serve in the defense of our country, women must carry on under difficult circumstances and they are an important factor in industry.

What kind of a job can women do; how important is the job and what will it mean to ourselves, to our families, and to our country? What are the responsibilities of government? How can we carry on a dual role of homemaker and worker? In emergency and of necessity it can and must be done, since our country has pledged commitments to the world. We have promised through the United Nations to destroy communism; to spread democracy and to help the weak nations throughout the world. This is a soul-stirring program and one which will require all we have to give of ourselves and the things that God has provided us in great abundance.

Though production of food and clothing has gone out of the home into the factories, we still depend upon women for much of the work connected with providing these essentials to American families. All the modern conveniences and the public services which contribute to our high standard of living and cultural advance require the work of women as well as of men. The electrical goods industry is one of the largest employers of women. It is always a woman's voice that answers our mechanized call for telephone service. We deal almost entirely with women clerks in department stores and elsewhere. In restaurants and hotels, in laundries and dry cleaning establishments, we find women working in large numbers. In our schools, our libraries, our museums, our publication plants, women are contributing to our cultural life. Women workers are found in practically every industry. Nearly a third of all the workers in the country in the year of 1951 were women. The role these women play in our present society is a significant one.

In our early-day economy, most of the work of providing for family needs was done at home. Our society was primarily rural, and both father and mother worked at home producing the things that the family used, with the help of sons and daughters. The woman's main contribution to this form of economy was in the daily tasks that she performed without financial remuneration. Even the teaching of the children was done by the mother at home.

Since then there has been a great change in the country's pattern of living. Home manufacturing became obsolete with the advent of the industrial revolution. Later inventions speeded up the processes of production and took from the home many of the time-consuming tasks which had occupied women. Home work was further cut down by modern labor-saving devices and by the growth of laundries, bakeries, and other labor establishments for providing outside help.

As the country became industrialized, more and more families moved to cities and the family-life pattern became primarily urban. Families who continued to live on the farm experienced a great change in their mode of living. The tractor and other modern farm machinery simplified the outdoor work, and rural electrification brought into the farm home many of the conveniences which lighten housework. The benefits of city shopping and other urban advantages were made available to farm families by the advent of the automobile.

The technological changes which took manufacturing out of the home and lightened housework for women created a demand for women workers in factories and industrial plants where the skills they had already cultivated could be used. The invention of the telephone started a new industry and the introduction of the typewriter created a demand for women in office work.

It follows naturally that women increasingly accepted the opportunity to work outside the home as a means of earning money.

The movement of women into industry was greatly accelerated by two world wars. World War I added to the variety of jobs women did in all types of factories, particularly in metal and machinery plants and other plants making war implements. It gave women the opportunity to do more types of skilled work than they had previously been allowed to undertake. Many women dropped out of these jobs after the end of the war, but some continued to work in large numbers and the variety of employment offered to women was greater than it had been before.

The Second World War brought an even greater need for women workers since victory in the highly mechanized struggle depended on this country's all-out production. In business and industry throughout the nation women were urgently needed to increase the total number of civilian workers, as well as to replace the vast numbers of men who were called into the armed forces.

World War II brought unusual opportunities for women in scientific and technical fields, and their work proved so valuable that industrial concerns continued to employ them in considerable numbers. In the business world, the shortage of men gave women a chance to move into positions of more responsibility, and the number of women in high-level jobs has continued to increase. In January 1951, almost a million women were working as managers, officials, and proprietors according to the Census Bureau, whether in their own business or in managerial positions in enterprises of other persons. This represented a gain of over 100,000 in the past two years.

In total numbers, there continued to be more women working after World War II than had been expected, and this was particularly true of older women many of whom had worked for the first time outside the home in war-time jobs and preferred to stay in the labor force. In the postwar period of full employment, there continued to be a need for women workers, and with prices of food, clothing, and other commodities remaining at high levels, the money received from outside work continued to draw them.

The national emergency caused by the United Nations' struggle to resist aggression in Korea increased the employment of women but not in the same way as World War II. The process was slower, since emergency conditions were not so acute as in the case of an all-out war. Defense mobilization did not reach the point where it changed the over-all picture of women's employment to any great extent.

There has been an increase of women in factory work. In a few women's specialty fields, such as nursing and secretarial, there is a shortage of workers. But in general, the labor supply for current military needs seems to be adequate, and recruitment of women for defense work is not imminent. However, if the present world emergency continues, the number of women workers can be expected to rise in proportion to the over-all effort. Women constitute the country's greatest labor reserve, and we know from experience that they can be counted on to readjust their lives to do whatever work is needed in times of national stress and danger.

While technological change and resultant economic pressure have been the major cause of the shift of women from home work to jobs in industry, the social factors related to women as human beings should not be overlooked in analyzing their progress and their place in today's industrialized society. Women, like men, have the fundamental urge for complete self-expression and a need to contribute to society by a full use of their education, experience, and talents. While the natural abilities of the majority find full expression in work connected with the home, there are others who find satisfactory outlet for their talents in employment. For individuals—either men or women—to be frustrated by being deprived of an opportunity to express their full personality through work they enjoy is recognized as detrimental to the individual and to society. It is therefore a healthy sign that our society has come to recognize the fact that women, as individuals, have the right to accept whatever job opportunities best fit their personal needs.

It has become customary in our society for women who are widowed, divorced, or separated from their husbands to seek employment outside the home, particularly if they are in need financially. This has been especially true when these women are mothers of small children in cases where the burden of supporting the children falls upon the mother.

Among married couples, and frequently among the newly married, it is not uncommon to find mutual expectation that husband and wife will share jointly in meeting expenses, particularly when special needs must be met and when the wife is reasonably free from child-caring responsibilities. In the years since World War II, thousands of young married veterans have been attending college or getting special training under the G.I. Bill of Rights, and this has meant, in many cases, that their wives have accepted full or part-time employment to supplement the small income provided by the United States Government to make this education possible.

It is far less customary or advisable for women with young children to work than for others, and only about 8 per cent of the women who work have children under six years of age. Most of the working women with children under school age are holding jobs because they need this income for their own and their children's support.

Looking back at the change in women's occupational status over the past fifty years, it is easy to see why women have become important in industry. They have successfully made the adjustment from a simple pioneer social order to a highly industrialized one. This adjustment has not been an easy one, for woman's role as homemaker has not been given up in this process nor should it ever be relinquished. When I think back over the years since my girlhood, I marvel at the difference these years have made in the situation faced then, and now, by a girl who starts out in the labor market.

I believe the first half of this century laid the foundation of our most progressive period. Some men still seem to have little confidence in women, particularly in important positions. However, the record proves that few women fail when given positions of responsibility. I believe they have gained immeasurably and will continue to gain in the years ahead. Women are working with men in business and the professions and are proving their ability. Most men who work with women now understand and respect not only their viewpoint but also their ability, courage, and integrity. It is to a great extent woman's own fault if she fails to receive recognition and respect.

This new status of woman embraces opportunities but also carries enormous responsibilities. The place of woman in business and industry is well established now and her contributions are known. However, as we survey the scene, can we be entirely content with the direction things are taking? Under pressure of crisis production, we must not lose our vision of the true woman nor allow our ideals and wisdom to be obscured. Increased production, high standards of living, material well-being should not be paid for with a defeminized womanhood. There is a tendency all over the world to magnify the value of production, organization, material might at the expense of human values. Efficiency and mass production cannot be considered the only goal. The effect on people of this production pressure has to be considered. For woman the real values are the human values. One of the most important challenges for women in the industrial field is to impress the primacy of human values. Production is for the sake of human beings and it should not destroy them in the process. The individuality of man and woman must not be surrendered to the insistence of unlimited production.

A stunning example of the loss of human value with strict adherence to equality in work production is told by Dr. Ada Halpern in her book on woman's *Liberation Soviet Style*.[1]

Obviously, the average woman can not lift as heavy a load, or hew as large an amount of coal as the average man. Therefore under the Soviet, she has either to earn less, or work longer. The tough appearance of these women doing heavy physical labor makes a deep impression on any person used to Western concepts; they are clad in rags, their feet are tied in bits of sacking, their hair is unkempt. Many look hardly like women at all.

Dr. Halpern says the men cursed and hit her when she was unable to pull her weight in the mine.

There is a growing tendency in our national life to measure the value of work in terms of financial return to the worker. This attitude reduces a worker to the level of a dray animal to be rewarded with a bundle of hay at the end of a day. The human values in work; the inherent power of the human being to master

[1] Ada Halpern, *Liberation Soviet Style*, London, MaxLove, 1945.

a material world; the development of individual talents and skills for the service of others; these are more spiritually rewarding than a weekly pay envelope bulging at the seams. Woman in industry must strive to preserve in this sphere of the American scene the spiritual and human value of work.

A national economic philosophy of greed and avarice can all too often be cloaked under a banner of humanitarianism. Higher material standards of living are desirable but only if they do not obscure or suppress the more valuable possessions of mind and spirit. It would be tragic in this country if woman, captivated by the desire for material things, became so dulled in spirit by her labor to gain them that she had no energy or interest left to give to things more truly feminine. Material well-being bought at the price of spiritual exhaustion or loss of interest is not worth the effort. Woman's presence and influence in the industrial scene, if she is true to her self, can keep it human. With her sense of the living person, her sympathy and compassion for the suffering, her sense of family life, she can temper the material attitudes that sometimes prevail in collective bargaining. In this connection one recalls an event in the life of Henry Ford. Mr. Ford had stubbornly closed his factories rather than submit to mediation with the C.I.O. organization. When he told his wife what he had done, this compassionate and strong-willed woman prevailed upon him to reopen the factories. Mr. Ford later explained why he had come to terms with the C.I.O., "Callie didn't want to see a lot of rioting and bloodshed because of the strike." A human value had prevailed over economic and material strife.

In this matter of her involvement in industry, woman should keep in mind whether she is surrendering to work for material advantages alone or whether she is correctly using work to make it serve her truly feminine purposes. Woman as an important part of the nation's work force must not forget that what may be required in crisis is not necessarily the normal thing. When crisis production tapers off, it will mean reduction of work force. In

91

The Spiritual Woman

such a situation woman will have to face a serious question. Will
it be better for her and for her country if she continues in the
work force, even though men are being laid off? It is more
devastating to the personality of a man to be unemployed than
it is to a woman. By nature, she can find many ways of self-
occupation and satisfaction which a man cannot. The idle man
deteriorates rapidly and the effect upon society of his deterioration is felt not only by his children but by future generations.

In an industrialized civilization, woman's spiritual influence
and emphasis are most needed to protect society against the
forces which are impersonal, mechanical, and materialistic. Such
a civilization presents a serious challenge to woman which she
must meet with clear vision, courage, and conviction.

IX

ELIZABETH S. RIDDER

Woman and Leisure

TO analyze leisure and how best to use it is to discover that
it involves all aspects of life—spiritual, intellectual, and physical. In this age, more and more women are conscious of the
importance of free time. History proves in succeeding cycles that
the human race has come a long way in material progress. The
present is so filled with unique and diversified advantages that
it is a distinctly new world—a world just dawning. The reason I
call ours "a world just dawning" is because of the new and
promised scientific developments, bringing about many changes
different from all other times and more directly affecting woman.
These developments, exerting tremendous influence, are not
always used in a way compatible with cultural advancement.
They can be a blessing or a menace to society.

The majority of men and women and their families have more
time on their hands than in other years because of labor-saving
devices and shorter working hours. But this free time is worthless
if the hours are misspent. As a people, have we drifted into
unplanned use of our leisure without concern about the
advantages or disadvantages of the diversions we choose? One
of the urgent challenges of our times is how we use our free
hours.

A country's standard of living shows its material growth but its degree of culture can be measured only by its intellectual and moral life. How leisure time is spent is a sign of the cultural level of a nation. History shows that whenever there is excessive absorption in material things, cultural decay is the more rapid. Therefore it is important that we rethink the purposes and values of leisure. So much of our increased leisure, made possible by great scientific and technological aids, is being squandered on little things by thoughtless people. There has been such emphasis on the acquisition of material goods for selfish use, many people have lost their sense of community responsibility. Woman, particularly, should carefully consider the value of her leisure time because this materialistic civilization can induce her to spend her free time on superficial, trivial, and material things. Not only can her own personality suffer by becoming superficial and materialistic, but society suffers too. If woman surrenders to superficiality, she can make no contribution to the elevation of the cultural and spiritual level of society. Of importance is how the leisure of woman may be less "of the world" and more "for the world." My own aim in this chapter is to probe the inner potentiality of leisure and the cultural influence it can foster.

The use of our free time may become a selfishness which enervates and corrupts, or it may contribute to the development of personality for the benefit of the community. Hours are wasted that are spent in passive submission to trite entertainment which distorts the true values of life. Such a leisure may help to pass time but it does not enrich the mind or broaden one's view of the real treasures of life. Life between periods of work is not just a game, but a challenge to the discovery of more exalted heights of living and an adventure in spiritual growth. If we occupied our leisure for self-centered satisfaction alone, it would be a denial of our civic and social responsibilities. We would then be refusing to give that extension of ourselves which is required for the enrichment of others. We personally gain, and society gains, as a result of generous association with other people in fulfilling civic and social duties.

So many people need recreation for relaxation, yet the purpose of free time is not solely recreation. The furious drive for recreation in American life more often results in exhaustion or depletion of our energies than in the refreshment of the body and the spirit which is recreation's true purpose. So much energy absorbed in aimless diversion leaves little for the pursuit of more valuable things. The external activities have been so magnified in the American scale of values that people feel guilty if they are not perpetually busy about external things. Even vacation time must be filled with a rush of activity. We seem to dread the tranquillity and silence that induce relaxation of mind and exaltation of spirit, which should be the goal of leisure. As it is, leisure too often revolves around other forms of labor and work as an interlude between hours and days of work. Rest and repose are looked upon as a waste of time that might better be used in doing things and producing something. Woman as a trustee of the future should be the first to urge that the activities which occupy so much of the nation's leisure time be such that they enrich our people culturally. It is more the mind and the spirit of America than the body and the senses that call for development and enrichment.

Let us go back to an earlier generation of woman. A backward glance will help to bring out the contrast as well as the permutation of activities. Those were the days when grandmother knew with an age-old wisdom that security began in the home with a sharing of spiritual and cultural things, and grandfather did his part to help her. How many accounts we find where grandfather gathered his family about him and read out loud from the Bible every evening. And grandmother's "leisure" is a chronicle of her family, her neighbors, her assistance to the needy, all of whom felt the radiation of her charity. When she wasn't doing the heavy chores of household duties, without any scientific inventions to help her, she devoted her leisure to her usual schedule;

visiting the sick and aged, sewing, crocheting, reading, church work, and best pleasure of all, extending her unselfish eagerness to welcome, to companion, to guide not only her own children but her grandchildren. So, grandmother's leisure was "a thing of beauty," the loveliness of unselfish service, a community asset bent on "leveling up" the lives around her, happy to bolster the courage of others through the warmth of her simple, direct faith and the extension of her mature personality to enrich society.

However acrimoniously and critically the lines were drawn on woman suffrage, I ask myself if there were not a noble impulse and hopeful thrust in the suffragette movement. It was to be a new use of leisure; woman in polemics, woman in public life, woman with an equal rights idea. The ladies in the vanguard may have felt that the industrial revolution—inventions, factory work, manufacture in leaps and bounds—was turning their world upside down. Woman suffrage could have been predicated on the expectation of improving conditions of the poor, of people working in the vast new empire of factories where employees' surroundings had not yet been thought out. But the vote for women met with such stormy opposition that bitterness crept in and the victory recorded naught of the subtle, higher aims.

World War I had the effect of prompting homebodies into group war work. The Red Cross did a painstaking job in enlisting woman's help in teaching and programming, and all at once the American woman knew what it meant to be a volunteer. This, to me, was the pivotal point at which women in larger ratios began to see their responsibility in the community. Forerunners to this were the small, faithful groups in the Ladies' Aid Society, the Children's Aid Society, Travelers' Aid, and other organizations setting a good example. At that time, too, the ground work and quiet steady growth of such organizations as Girl Scouting were coming along, channeling woman's service to the extent that at present there are 500,000 volunteers in Scouting. These women have dedicated their leisure time to the delicate duty of guiding one million and a half young people whose pledge begins:

> On my honor, I will try:
> To do my duty to God and my country . . .

I cite the example of Scouting because I have worked with it for a long time. It tends toward the total aspects of leisure on a high plane because it distributes the adult's leisure in the kindly direction of young people's leisure. Its programming is a far cry from that of the mothers who either buy or allow their children to fill free time with the reading of cartooned stories that go under the misnomer of comics. Parents with refined and cultured interests will give to society, children who have developed good tastes and exalted interests. The beautiful, the true, and the good are still the yardsticks of culture. True parenthood does not confine its vision to physical and material wellbeing. Its greatest privilege is the formation of the minds and the development of a sense of values in children. The human mind and spirit are precious gifts which have capacity for growth. It takes time outside of domestic chores and the physical aspects of child-raising to exercise the privilege of forming children culturally. Surely women with their new leisure will want to dedicate a good share of it to the cultural formation of the young. Because of increased incomes of the average American family, many have been catapulted into substantially higher levels of living. It is especially important that children are not spoiled by sudden wealth. In this group, particular attention will want to be given to the formation of the character of the child. Although he may be taught manners to match his new standard of living, yet what of his character? A common error in values is to confuse culture with manners. It is too easy to be satisfied with a veneer of manners without realizing that behind this veneer many unrefined personalities are hidden. Young people today, whose lives have been surrounded with material protection and concessions, show an emotional and intellectual immaturity that later expresses itself in general irresponsibility. They expect society to entertain and care for them as their parents did. They have not been taught to use their leisure time wisely but have been allowed to drift from one game to another, from one distraction to another, and they emerge from home into community life indifferent, uninterested in others, and looking only for selfish advantages.

We are beginning to realize, more and more, the importance of teaching our young that the advantages of our society are due to the work, energy, and dedication of many people who dared to use their time properly and to assume responsibility, as our grandparents did. So large a percentage of the population has been coasting along on the spiritual strength of their forebears! Women who remember the spiritual teaching of their grandparents have so neglected it they can't even define it and consequently their children have less church affiliation and sensitivity to the spiritual than they. This lack of strength in spiritual guidance is becoming a block to the deeper personal good and the larger community good.

The days which followed World War I were promising and exciting. Leisure time was a gay, almost irresponsible affair and it "jazzed" its way right up to the depression. A right-about-face after the 1929 crash bolted thinking and living into stern reality, the growing trend toward materialism was set back, young women couldn't afford to finish college, resourcefulness was the watchword as necessity held the reins. The 1930's taught many a good lesson. The ads in those days started counseling "It's Smart to Be Thrifty." Leisure swerved to self-improvement, people concentrated on "how to win friends," picture puzzles were engrossing grownups—fitting pieces together into an integrated whole was perhaps prognostic of the national dilemma.

World War II in the 1940's had the immediate effect of reminding woman that an hour or two of leisure time could be applied usefully. An increase in registrations began in voluntary services. It was then discernible that woman, who had been endowed by

98

modern society with more freedom and leisure, had a real contribution to make to the kind of life that was emerging. Civilian participation in two world wars introduced a more sensitive concept of leisure activity to woman. From home, office, and classroom, she came with whatever free hours she had to volunteer in hospitals, in local and national civic groups, with the gratifying result that when the wars were over, the conscientious participant relinquished the work reluctantly. Some, it must be noted, continued or found other avenues of service. Parenthetically, if civic and private agencies had been able to program these volunteer hours immediately into peace-time services in nursery and foundling groups through to old-age groups, the picture of leisure with a spiritual note of unselfishness might now be a shining beacon, a *fait accompli*.

These "stepping stones" of leisure since the early 1900's have led us in many directions. Fifty years later, leisure is a vast circle with radii of multiple attractions and of multiple possibilities. Recognition of these new frontiers of leisure opens an encouraging vista on this "new world dawning." There are many organizations on the local level which are planned to serve the needs of individual communities. If a woman is not willing to give some of her leisure to the activities of these groups, she curtails their productive and effective work. And what affects our community life affects us individually. Should not woman, then, study the local scene, pinpoint its problems, think out the solutions, and act in concert with other women? We never know what talent we can have at times, until we are challenged to the use of it. Every mind has the capacity for some advance and it is a misuse of leisure to neglect this distinctive human gift. To fill leisure time properly in group work requires preparation. It is no longer enough to dash in with time on your hands and a willingness to help. It must not be haphazard, nor is it advisable to select a community activity that is a hardship. The head and the heart must go with the plans for a better leisure. It requires using your head—thinking out which activity will bring out your own potential for the benefit of the community. Will you go simply, kindly, without selfish motive, to channel your energy into efforts toward a total good? Will you remember *not* to sweep your friends into the work before you determine whether their potential lies in the same area? There are many cultural opportunities in all communities—schools, adult education, book review forums, clubs, and libraries. There is the wide area of religious study groups which foster renewal of the daily reading of the Bible, a practice which should again be welcomed in every home. A consideration of leisure activities unequivocally focuses our minds on the deeper meaning of life. The habit of living intensely, of courting anxiety, of being caught in a frenzy of busyness seems to command the reevaluation of the necessity of a purpose, even in free time.

The continuous pressure of modern production can deaden the spirit of mankind and it is for woman to help relax this intensity of external effort by guiding human beings to a more vigorous sponsorship of valuable interests to fill leisure time. We must rediscover the satisfactions and delights of a leisure spent in the nourishment of spiritual and cultural values. If we make this rediscovery of the value of leisure, it will contribute much to the spiritual revitalization of our country.

> The world is too much with, us; late and soon,
> Getting and spending, we lay waste our powers.
> —WILLIAM WORDSWORTH

N.B. A list of community organizations which welcome volunteer assistance from qualified married and single women, and other suggestions for filling free time has been prepared by the author and is available without charge. Address your request to the Editor, in care of the publisher.

X

HELEN C. WHITE

Woman in Literature

WE Americans are taking justifiable pride in the increasing recognition which our literature is receiving all over the world. We are delighted to hear, for instance, that our writers have a considerable following in Europe. Many of them we are proud to have as our cultural spokesmen, and we rejoice in the honor they have brought us. But there are others of whom we can say only that we should be sorry if people in other countries whose good opinion of us is of national interest should think we are really like that.

It is one of the extraordinary consequences of the realistic or naturalistic movement in writing that, whatever its original intention, much of its product is fantasy of an unpleasant kind. In a way it is a tribute, albeit an indirect one, to the reality of our everyday American world that a sensation-craving age should be so driven to express itself. I recall a brilliant pair of sophomores I once had in a writing course who were delightful themselves and turned out to be fine and distinguished men; but to judge from the stories they wrote, they came from an incredible background in which madness, suicide, and murder seemed to be the normal human expectation. When I finally saw the place where they came from, I was astonished to find a peaceful river town, rimmed with golden fields and low blue-green hills rolling along the horizon. These embryonic writers had been treating me to an epitome of all the horror and violence that had ever befallen the town in a hundred years of not only its modest history, but also of the village gossip, that ancient form of folk art that dwarfs all sophisticated literary effort when it comes to the lurid and the mysterious.

No one is trying to hide the fact that terrible things happen in our fortunate land. One has only to read the newspapers for the external lineaments of crime and weakness, and folly and mischance. It takes no very sensitive imagination to realize the inward agonies mercifully hidden from the average tabloid fancy. But these things do not happen that often, nor with quite that much density to the square inch. It is the concentrated essence of human weakness and misery that we are revealing in so much of our literature today that is unfortunate. One cannot help wondering about the human factor behind such unsparing concentration. Didn't the sunshine fall on the typewriter once in all those long days? Did no bird sing in that airtight neighborhood? Didn't that ascetic, of all ascetics, look up into a single smiling face all those dreary months in which he wrought so patiently to demonstrate that hell is not only hereafter?

If we are to take some of our contemporary writers at their word, they certainly do not seem to know the right kind of women. It is difficult to fathom how so many of them could know, even on the law of averages, so many of the wrong sort. However, it is not only the immoral, or amoral, or premoral, women who are often found in contemporary fiction and drama. In many of the transactions and settings which some literary imaginations seem to haunt, it would be hard to find any good or even supermoronic women. In many of these situations the apparent heroines are depicted not so much as human beings, but as passive complements, or even props, to the main action. As that rises somewhat muggily from the sensory to the reflective level, these so-called heroines retreat even further from independent reality and become mere embodiments of the main ego's psychological hangover, and projections of his own sobering self-distaste. If the creators of these plastic women figures were given to discrimination, or recognized the importance of fairness and frankness to honesty, we should probably not have to worry. But there is always that hasty impulse to the unscientific generalization.

On the other hand, when such an author does embark on developing a characterization of a good woman, the result is almost worse. His conventionally good woman is presented in such a way as to make goodness itself dull and unappetizing. There are all the triangle wives, the moms, the presidents of the ladies' auxiliaries, etc. If these good women do embody, in any round and humanly variegated fashion, folly, vanity, and drive for power, they seem to have at least the chastening effect of any serious presentation of the all too familiar evil. But when we find that the best love of which even a mediocre spirit is capable yields not even a moment's insight or tenderness, but only folly and weakness, and the poor heart's best receives only the contempt of superior knowledgeableness, then the effect is close to blasphemy. And there I think we should give over the argument, and simply ask, "Is that the best you can offer us?" There is no reason why any of us should keep such poor company.

These portrayals of women irritate any self-respecting woman, but they are no more objectionable than another type which is too often simply overlooked. This type portrays a conception of woman which is not so much presented as tacitly taken for granted. This portrayal occurs in much of the "literature" addressed to women by supposedly respectful writers, including not only men but women, too. I refer to a type of writing offered by newspapers and magazines, by radio and movies. This literature is written for the average woman and is sponsored by advertising agencies that, however they may sniff at the old saw about the hand that rocks the cradle, are aware of the hand that fills the wire cart in the super-market. This writing is supposed to be about good women for good women. As one thwarted young

Jeremiah once wrote to me at the end of his first year after graduation, when only his wife's typewriter kept the wolf from the door, "We are eating again. I am writing stories about nice-girl-meets-nice-boy under circumstances that even you would approve of." There is nothing wrong with the scenario; in fact the future of the race depends on it! But too often the women involved and the women addressed are taken as a matter of course to be silly, gullible, and sentimental; to be without enough mind or moral sense to know whether what they are reading or listening to makes any sense, or any difference in any real world.

What can we do about it? There is one thing we can do easily but will not if we are wise, and that is to set up an external code of moral standards and regulations and try to apply them in a wholesale fashion. We can make some topics taboo, and insist that when other topics are handled, they be handled in a certain way. We can set certain limits to description and imagery, and forbid the use of certain words and terms. That sort of thing has been attempted often in whole or in part, and in various places and under various conditions, so that we have experience to judge by. It does not work well in the short run, and it could be disastrous in the long run, as we Americans should know from our own literary history.

A study of the artistic development of some of our best-known realistic and naturalistic writers makes certain points clear. The first is that any setting up of standards demands a wide view of the area of experience to be ordered, and requires sound judgment on the part of the lawgiver, neither so common as to be taken for granted. Morality is more than a hatred of evil: it is a love of goodness. Fear is not enough; faith is indispensable. Zeal does not suffice without charity. And judgment rests on honesty and humility. It is simple to let convention take over and retreat to the false security of a black and white point of view, trusting to vague idealism to blur the harsh edges. The result is often sentimentalism, harmless enough in itself perhaps, but inviting complacency and hypocrisy. Such restriction soon creates its own vacua of curiosity, if nothing more, and literary sentimentalism becomes self-destructive. The taste which it has failed to educate (and imagination and emotion need cultivation no less than the logical faculties) is left exposed to all the shoddy deceits of the various brands of sensationalism. The result is a kind of naïve and gullible public that is ready to swallow the most banal revelation if it is presented sensationally enough, and that all too often can be persuaded to believe that puerile indecency is frankness, and uncontested sensuality, passion. Out of the nineteenth-century post-Puritan reading public came the twentieth-century public for the naturalistic writers.

Such naturalism is not good for the public, and it is bad for the writer, as anyone knows who has read the biographies of the leaders of the realistic and naturalistic schools, or who has watched the youthful imitators of these masters find their own feet on far from level ground. The kind of young man who writes is likely to be in any age a human being of keen sensibilities and of inflammable imagination. It would be a mistake to say that he is maladjusted by nature. But something usually has made him stop, look, and listen while his contemporaries more or less unconsciously drift along. When one looks back at the youth of many American writers, it is interesting to note how many of them began with some kind of revolt against their environment. Sometimes it was just the bareness and bleakness of a raw new frontier world; sometimes it was the narrowness and tacit rigidity of a not so new world, which had perhaps somewhat prematurely solidified. Sometimes it was a more complicated situation. The young man came to resent the socially reinforced grip of a religious orientation which had not in any effective fashion commanded his personal interest or concern, or he came to despise a religious tradition, into the riches of which he had never really entered. Sometimes he revolted against misery and sometimes against prosperity. And in a society like ours, in which the pursuit of wisdom and beauty is not generally accorded the regard commanded by the pursuit of wealth or power, the effect of all these rebellions is intensified, so that the normal self-assertiveness of youth is brought to the explosive point.

The predicament of the young writer in a by no means "young world" should never be forgotten. It would seem that all he had to do was to get up on the shoulders of his predecessors and do what they had done as well as it could be done, and certainly in all but a few ages of the world's history better than it was done. I have heard that formula offered to account for Shakespeare's success. Even if this were true, it would not help much, for the simple reason that there are not many Shakespeares. The young writer's chances of doing what everybody else is doing, better than anybody else, are practically nonexistent, in the beginning at least. The chances of his superiority being immediately recognized are not much better. The tendency of the young writer, therefore, is to try to carry something that has already been done further than it has gone before. In other words, h- has to yell to make himself heard above the crowd. In a sensational age, his temptation is to be more sensational than the rest. It does little good for a world whose morality he does not respect to tell him that he is immoral. He will take such censure as fresh proof of the world's wrongness and a vindication of his own rightness.

The fruitful approach to this problem is a basic one. Before we try to set up standards for literature, we need to ask ourselves what it is that we want of literature, what is its place in our scheme of things, individual and collective, and then what is the excuse for being of the particular work under consideration. Most sophisticated people will agree that literature is a good thing, even if they do not have much time for it. Books are one of the ways of "keeping up," if only through the club book report, or the newspaper book review. But most Americans think of literature as a leisure-time activity; something for recreation. That would not be so bad if our hard-driving, production-centered civilization had a high idea of recreation and its place in human life, but it hasn't. Even in quarters which have emancipated themselves from Puritan faith and Puritan ethics, there is a survival of the middle-class Puritan bad conscience about pleasure. But now it takes a secularized form. It hasn't a sense of sin any more, but rather a self-condescending sense of self-indulgence. Something of the self-disprizing in the indulgence transfers itself to the means and the source of the means. The half-conscious awareness that an author, as a type, is outside of the tribal bounds produces that good-humored refusal to take literature seriously that is common in our society.

Literature is, to be sure, a source of entertainment, of delight, and of refreshment. These are good things not to be undervalued in a world like the one we live in. But literature is more than that. At its best it stimulates the imagination and it enlarges the sympathies of the individual human being. We spend ingenuity in developing the body of man and in training his mind. We do a good deal, though obviously not enough, in training the will. But too often we leave the emotions to take care of themselves in a welter of exaggerated and irrelevant appeals splashed in sound and color all over our landscape. We forget that the imagination is more than daydreaming or wishful thinking. There is no resource of the human personality that cannot be blunted or stunted by neglect, or dissipated and wasted by abuse, and this is preeminently true of the imagination and the emotions. There can be health and tone of both the imaginative and the emotional life, and literature can serve to develop it. There is nothing like good company to help in this area, and good writers are that, with the added availability of uncommon articulateness.

Literature can widen our horizons. Human life is larger than the experience of any one of us, and no one would knowingly remain imprisoned within himself. Literature can help us to an understanding of ourselves and of others and between these understandings there is an interaction that enriches both. Literature can help us to penetrate the meaning of our lives, to give body and substance to our values and ideals, to reach toward those things that are beyond our human limitations. There are more things in heaven and on earth than are dreamed of in the philosophy of any of us. Literature may serve to open our hearts and minds to them. Human life in any age is a fever and a fret without time and will for contemplation, and the spirit fails for breath.

It is in the light of this conception of literature and its function that we focus on woman's relation to it. So far we have been referring to those things that are the business of the human spirit, shared by both sexes, the common ground of humanity.

But limitation is the mark of man's life on this earth, limitation of senses, of attention, of energy. Selection, choice, and conversely rejection are the first conditions of any effective dealing with human problems. Especially is this true when it comes to doing the world's work. The training and habit that make a man able to do one job make him less ready to do a number of others, and prolonged devotion to one job completes the specialization.

It is this fact that makes the basic specialization of man's and woman's work in the world at once so inescapable and so difficult to assess. Men and women, different in physical endowments from the beginning, have different jobs to do in the never-ending work of carrying on the human race. But whatever the relative parts which endowment and nature play in the development of the mature man and woman, there is no question of the actuality of the resulting differences. They are considerable enough to justify the general norms of masculine and feminine, essential to the maintenance of the fabric of society. So essential, in fact, that any society with margin enough for self-reflection has been explicit in developing them, and any society secure in its standards resolute in enforcing them. In other words, of their practical usefulness for the fulfillment of the tasks of men and women on this earth, there can be no question! But, of course, like everything human they exact the price of limitation.

Following the feminist movement of the nineteenth and

twentieth centuries thoughtful people, at least, were aware of the violence which that enforcement had done to individual talent and interest in the case of women. The varieties of reaction to the feminist movement which we see in our day are proof of the impression which feminism has made. But there has been no comparable growth in the general appreciation of what the processes of this social standardization have done to masculine differences. The masculine woman is viewed variously with amusement or horror, but I doubt if either view is as absolute as the contempt which society has for the feminine man. The restrictions on feminine boldness and aggressiveness are certainly no more frustrating than are the pressures, tacit and overt, brought to bear on masculine sensitiveness and compassion. The cruelty of society in enforcing rigid norms of behavior is well understood today in America, to no small extent because of the memory of the not so remote rebellion against the extremes of Puritanism. But the possible destructiveness of such cruelty is still far from appreciated. It is a pity that men should think of "feminine" as a term of reproach to a super-sensitive man, but tragic that women should ever, even with tongue in cheek, echo that contempt and unknowingly rob an artistic temperament of talent and confidence.

But from the woman's point of view, which is the main concern of this book, the most egregious example of an underprizing of woman's role is the common attitude toward the role of the housewife, which is woman's primary calling. It is hard to understand the popular condescension toward the many-faceted, many-skilled job of the homemaker. If there are children in the home, then I wonder how many of us concentrated, canalized specialists think we should survive a week of such manifold responsibility and distraction! When one remembers that today's failures in the home cannot be shuffled off to the next expert, but will be there for tomorrow and for years of tomorrows, one cannot help wondering whoever invented the term "a mere housewife."

It is time that we faced the fact that in spite of all the

standardization of our mass-production civilization, there are fortunately still a good many different human situations, and many different approaches to them. It is important that we should respect these differences, and a good place to begin is with the most obvious one of all, the difference between men and women. For though we do have the same general spiritual problems, there are differences due to the differing experiences of our ways of life. We do well to seek to enlighten and to complement each other, but never to undervalue or contemn. For we need each other's respect and sympathy if we are each to do our proper share for the common good.

We need to understand each other and that is where literature, working as it should, imaginatively and emotionally as well as intellectually, can help. For that reason it is important that women do their share of serious writing. There is no reason why they should confine themselves to feminine themes or spheres, any more than man should keep within his masculine scope. But it would be a pity if woman did not use her interior knowledge of a woman's world for artistic purposes. After all, half the living of the world is done by women in women's situations and predicaments, with women's resources. Men should be encouraged to explore, not to exploit that world, and women should give them help. Of course, unfortunately woman can do what she has often done in literature and in other fields, and that is imitate what men have done without asking herself if that is what a woman would do. If she does that, she will probably receive a prompt response to and ready understanding of what she has produced, but she will add very little to the total situation.

It is not enough to have a good theme or wide experience in the area chosen to write a book. It is not enough to have a sense of mission. Writing demands more than that of man or woman. It takes a sustained devotion, in which women are usually strong, and a great concentration, which woman, by nature, does not usually possess. One will seldom find a woman,

110

even in student days, with that ruthless disregard of every other obligation and every other consideration, with that driving passion to get a particular poem or play or story completed that will make a young man shut himself up for hours and even days, and throw everything he has into the one job. It does not become any easier for woman to do this when she has taken on the responsibilities of mature life. However, the wrestling with difficulties, the driving against odds is the very nature of the artistic undertaking. Some women at least should make the attempt. To mention only two, Willa Cather and Sigrid Undset, in different ways, showed what can be done.

The attempt may be made on various levels and in a number of modes. Not many women, nor men for that matter, will be naturally equipped to attempt anything so central as Willa Cather's best work, or so broad and powerful as Sigrid Undset's. But there are other models. Jane Austen cannot be forgotten. Compared with what is available to many modern women, her education was limited and casual. Her experience was provincial, and her social range from our point of view incredibly narrow. She seems not so much indifferent to the larger movements of her age as completely unaware of them. Her interests were confined to human character and human relations and human behavior under commonplace circumstances, but in her penetration of what she saw in her limited theater, she went to the heart of many things in human life that are still valid for a different world, more than two centuries later! She was, in her quiet way, a wise woman, in nothing wiser than in the instrument she chose, a keen but unpretentious humor. The very modesty of her undertaking made possible a perfection of achievement that still holds the admiration of all who know art when they see it.

But few women will feel the call to write in comparison with those who read and talk about what they read. The importance of the women for whom men have written literature is abundantly witnessed to in many times and places. When in the eighteenth

111

century, Addison was trying to rouse the often frivolous women of the newly enriched middle class of England to a greater interest in self-cultivation, he reprinted a tribute which a seventeenth-century poet had written to a famous patroness of letters, the then Dowager-Countess of Pembroke:

> Underneath this marble hearse
> Lies the subject of all verse
> Sidney's sister, Pembroke's mother:
> Death, ere thou hast killed another,
> Fair and learned, and good as she,
> Time shall throw a dart at thee.

The intervening three hundred years since those lines were written have swept away the patronage system and not many who read these lines have the means to give fine literature the full financial support it sorely needs. But the poorest of us has still the patronage to bestow of the book she chooses to read and to recommend to her friends. One of the most active patronesses I know is a busy mother of five children who has found time to get a parish library under way and see that it is used.

To be such a patroness requires, of course, taste and judgment, and they are not easily come by. But any woman who takes her personal reading as the responsibility it is can make a beginning. There is a good deal of help available in the reviews of the more serious newspapers and periodicals. There is a considerable body of literary criticism to which any good library will give an introduction. But nothing is so conducive to the formation of good taste as the experience of reading good literature and thinking about it. And here reading and study groups will bring the added stimulation of the exchange of ideas. The woman who will take the trouble to make intelligent use of such aids can be effective in helping to create a reading public that will ignore the kind of literature that satisfies none of us and encourage every serious effort in the direction of the literature we want.

XI

SISTER ELIZABETH KENNY
AND
VALERIE HARVEY [1]

Woman in Nursing

"WE are put on this earth for a special destiny. Simply, it is our destiny to do the work of God. Each finds his way to do that work. If we live up to it, all is well here and hereafter. If we cannot rise to our destiny, if we cannot withstand the tests given us to strengthen our soul, we are disconsolate. Inwardly, some people know or sense this discord, and that is the greatest unhappiness in the world, just as living up to our purpose is the greatest joy. I recognized this and made my choice.

"Many women fear being a spinster and dread the label of being an 'old maid.' All the world rightly extols and sanctifies the state of holy matrimony and motherhood. But as a young girl I discovered for myself the call of devoting oneself entirely to God. This I chose early and happily, probably because I found my work early.

"Just as enforced poverty often brings out the worst in people, so does unwanted bachelorhood or spinsterhood rouse bitterness

[1] Editor's note: Sister Kenny died before her work for this chapter was completed. Her protégée, Valerie Harvey, includes the following excerpts from an article by Sister Kenny.

113

and restless frustration in one. But there is supreme nobility in *chosen* poverty. Pierre and Madame Curie refused riches as have hundreds of scientists, research workers and others who work to aid mankind and better the world. Freedom, dignity and fulfillment are in the single life *only* when dedication inspires it and solo living is a definite decision.

"My life is a prayer, day and night, given unreservedly to God. I wake in the morning to place myself at His service and command. I know I am doing His work as He guides me, and gives me the necessary strength, knowledge, patience and inspiration.

"I have been blessed with many remarkable answers to prayer, as has anyone whose daily living is a prayer. When I miss receiving answers and guidance, I know I have failed somewhere and am quick to recheck myself—to go back for a dropped stitch, so to speak, even if it means ripping out a long piece of living. . . .

"My work ties in very closely with the nursing profession which is handicapped today by a shortage of nurses. Yet a few generations ago almost every little girl dreamed at one time of becoming a nurse and succoring sufferers.

"The nursing profession was founded by a woman, Florence Nightingale, who was the most envied of every woman in the world. Universally, girls instinctively knew that the only satisfactory life is a life of service—and that perhaps the greatest possible service to humanity is to the sick. They knew instinctively that no other career could hold the rewards of life-saving, of restoration and healing.

"This world today, we all know, is sick, chaotic and on the verge of madness. Somewhere along the line, the nursing profession, too, became overinvolved with selfish rather than selfless standards. One needs a living wage, but where is the guiding star of nobility that inspired girls to look upon nursing as something far more than a job?

"I've talked with so many nurses who protest that patients regard them as glorified personal maids. I feel it is up to the nurses themselves to establish the dignity of their calling. They are servants of God. Their attitude and behavior can make their work so recognized.

"I believe the girls of the world can do no greater service to civilization than to return the nursing profession to the holy and blessed status of dedication. Anything to do with life and death is a cornerstone of the world serenity and strength. The principles of the medical profession are intertwined with religion and have been the highest and most respected in all races and creeds. These principles need to be vitalized, demanded by nurses themselves and lived up to so that nursehood is a privilege as well as a job.

"To a good doctor there is nothing more beautiful than a true nurse, who faithfully carries out her duty in a Christ-like work. And there is no profession, that so closely follows in the footsteps of Christ, as the work of healing—whether that man or woman be Christian, Jew, heathen or Oriental." [2]

As Sister Kenny has said, nature from birth has prepared woman for one of her most natural roles, that of nursing. Caring for the sick, the mentally ill, and the physically handicapped has appeal to woman because she has been endowed with a talent for sympathy, compassion, and understanding of personal human relationship. Many of us know a woman who, without benefit of formal nursing training, has successfully cared for someone she loved during an illness and brought him back into the family circle. She had nothing but natural instincts to guide her, but what amazing results she obtained by using her inherent qualities.

The professional nurse of course needs to develop fully these natural qualities of woman if she is to become a success in her profession. She becomes skilled in her profession by many years of study, training, and experience. But no matter what academic background a nurse may have, if she ever submerges womanly

[2] Excerpts from article by Sister Kenny in *Guideposts,* published at Pawling, N.Y.

qualities, she will not be a good nurse. Indeed, she will be a machine-like creature, poorly carrying out the bare necessities of her job.

The medical knowledge which the professional nurse obtains during her nursing education should combine with her natural talents. Never should a nurse become mechanical and impersonal in her ministrations to the sick. She must be dependable but never coldly efficient, firm but never hard, competent but never arrogant, cheerful but never rowdy, poised but never condescending. She must be honest and have integrity but not cold, heartless, and automatic in her relationship with her patient. She must remember that her patient is a human being and, although at times he may seem querulous and overdemanding, she must remember that he is beset by many fears and misgivings. All patients are apprehensive that they may not make a recovery. A child must adjust to many strange people and his little mind is often in a turmoil of bewilderment wondering why his loved ones have deserted him to strangers. A mother can be filled with anxiety wondering if her family is being adequately cared for during her enforced absence. A father can have the added dread of financial obligations.

A good nurse does more than minister to the daily physical needs of her patient. She is responsible for his mental and spiritual well-being and for harmony between the patient and his family and friends. She must at all times have a cordial and friendly relationship with her fellow workers. These things cannot be learned from any textbook; they spring from the core of woman. The helpful knowledge obtained from textbook and lecture room is the means a nurse can use to emphasize her own natural womanly talents.

A nurse's role is not only one of giving. She does remarkably well on the receiving end too, but not necessarily in a monetary or material way. Although the present salary of a nurse is adequate to allow her to live moderately well, it could never put her in a high income bracket. Nevertheless, she is recompensed

116

in countless ways above the receiving of cash. In many intangible ways that can be measured in terms of spiritual gain, she is repaid for her untiring efforts, her constant vigilance, her patience, her interest and understanding, and her competent ministration of the nursing arts.

What a wonderful feeling of fulfillment it is for a nurse to know that she is capable of rendering a service to some unfortunate victim of a disease! What deep contentment she derives from knowing that her job has been well done! How humble, yet how joyously gratified, she feels because of the appreciation of her patient. What natural pleasure it gives her to know that by rendering a service to the public, she is held in high esteem by her fellow citizens.

Apart from technical medical knowledge a nurse finds that her profession is constantly teaching her a wonderful philosophy of life and an emotional and spiritual discipline. These priceless assets will bring her future happiness whether she uses them to advantage in her profession or to become a more understanding and tolerant friend, a better wife and mother. From the fortitude and courage continually being shown by her patients, she learns to go forth and meet her own setbacks and hardships with a stout heart.

Perhaps you have never thought of nursing as being particularly exciting. But it is. What excitement could equal the ushering into the world of a new-born babe, or the discharging of a patient completely recovered? If it is drama you seek, then the nursing field abounds with it. The drama of the operating room and the almost miraculous results of some of the new "wonder" drugs provide an ever exciting stimulus. If it is a challenge you look for, then nursing provides it! It challenges you as a woman and as a nurse, and if you can meet this, you will find yourself developing intellectually and spiritually. You will become a better woman and a better nurse. Perhaps you like travel. If you have graduated from an approved school of nursing, you can travel almost anywhere and always find employment. Perhaps you are married with grown children and you wish to continue working and run your home, too. Nursing, with its shift work, makes this possible.

The field of nursing is a unique school for the development of humanitarian qualities, the breaking down of prejudice and the building up of tolerance. Sickness and disease know no barriers, respect no persons. A nurse grows to understand that people are fundamentally alike, irrespective of their race, color, or creed, whether they are rich or poor, educated or illiterate, and that a human life is worth fighting for no matter from what social sphere it comes.

No one is exempt from the need of nursing care during his span of life, even if it is only the help given at our entrance into this world and the care to ease our passing.

No matter what personal gain and satisfaction a nurse reaps from her service to the sick, she must live a normal, well-balanced life. She cannot give her best to her patients unless she does. This she is now able to do because of the better working conditions of nursing, with shorter hours and increased pay, which give her a sense of security. She can join in diversified activities during her off-duty hours.

There is always a demand for nurses and it seems there always will be. Today the number of nurses is greater than ever before. However, as the supply increases, so does the demand. Never has the health of a nation been so well cared for. Centers for the prevention of disease have been set up. Well-baby clinics have been established, hospitals admit more patients, the population is ever increasing, industry has expanded its nursing facilities and more nurses are needed for civil defense and the armed services.

Every woman does not develop all the qualities needed to make a good nurse. Unfortunately, many have allowed themselves to become frustrated by the setbacks of life. They have developed warped attitudes toward troubles of their own and of others, or they have become maladjusted and excessively neurotic. Some are so selfish in the pursuit of their own pleasure that they have lost the qualities that make it possible to give themselves in a service to others. Any woman, married or single, who has developed her inherent qualities of sympathy, mother-love, affection, compassion, and understanding, who is willing to serve others, who is not afraid of hard work, who has the intellectual requirements for concentrated study, who appreciates serious responsibility, who is observant and can use quick intelligent judgment, who is dependable and of high integrity, and who genuinely likes and enjoys cooperating with people will make a good nurse.

To become a registered professional nurse, it is necessary to graduate from an approved school of nursing and pass a licensing examination. These schools of nursing vary somewhat in their requirements for admission but at least graduation from high school is necessary and, in some instances, one or more years of college is required. The minimum age for students is usually seventeen years and the maximum thirty-five years for enrollment in any professional nursing school.

After graduation, the nursing field offers many opportunities to the registered nurse. The positions available are plentiful and diversified. As a student nurse, she will have spent some time gaining experience in all kinds of nursing and at the time of graduation she may already be convinced that she is best suited for a particular type of nursing. For the most part, nurses prefer to gain more experience as a graduate doing general duty in a hospital before making a decision to branch out into any special field of nursing.

Nurses have availed themselves of the opportunity of taking advanced study and of gaining extra clinical experience in almost all diseases, and in preventive protection of the public health and in nursing education. The most common clinical fields a nurse specializes in are medical, surgical, pediatric, orthopedic, obstetric, and psychiatric nursing. Some choose to attend the Sister Kenny Foundation in courses for the registered nurse or registered physical therapist not over forty years of age, who is interested in both the nursing of poliomyelitis in the acute and convalescent stages and in the neuro-muscular retraining to insure maximum development of normal patterns of motion. As 75 per cent of polio victims are children, it is most essential for anyone interested in this work to have a love and understanding of children. A great emotional force surrounds polio, because of the fear that its victim may be left crippled. The graduate Kenny therapist not only must be an expert in the treatment of poliomyelitis in all its phases, but must be capable of using good psychology in dealing with her patient, offering him continual encouragement, understanding, and interest. She must be able to inspire confidence and faith in both patient and parent. She is well rewarded by the gratitude of patients and the knowledge that she has helped so many of them to return to a normal way of life.

Many women find satisfaction in public health nursing, the service which takes a nurse into the home of a patient. The type of patient the public health nurse treats does not require hospitalization and needs only part-time nursing care. The public health nurse deals not only with the care of the sick, but also with the prevention of disease, and with any factor that may threaten the social and physical well-being or the healthful living conditions of the people of her community. The public health nurse is called upon to use her initiative, to be resourceful and observing. As a woman and nurse, she must be able to convince people that her suggestions are for their own good and the good of the community.

Private duty nursing appeals to woman and the supply of private duty nurses available is never enough to fill the demand for their services. With only one patient to look after, either in the home or in the hospital, the private duty nurse can give more personal and satisfying care to her patient than if he were just one of many in a busy hospital ward. She has time to give him all the individual attention that a sick person craves, to discover the source of his fears and misgivings and to help him to overcome them.

Universities, colleges, boarding schools, nursery schools, and schools for crippled and handicapped employ nurses both to safeguard the health of their pupils and to administer to those who are sick. Because the educational standards in nursing have risen, more nurses wish to continue after graduation their education in a chosen field. The demand for teachers in the field of nursing education has increased considerably.

The number of nurses employed by industrial and business firms is increasing rapidly. In this field the nurse not only gives emergency care to any victim of injury, accident, or illness, but educates the workers to protect themselves against occupational hazards and promotes the maintenance of general good health.

A nurse has the opportunity of rendering a true patriotic service to her country. She can join one of the branches of the armed services; the Army Nurse Corps, the Navy Nurse Corps, or the Air Force Nurse Corps. In times of war the demand for nurses in the armed services is greatest, but even in peacetime, hospitals are maintained for the care of members of the armed services and their families.

There is need and opportunity for trained practical nurses. Because the registered nurse spends so much of her time carrying out the highly specialized techniques of treatment, many hospitals and institutions have found the trained practical nurse invaluable. She carries out the general nursing care of patients not critically ill, under the supervision of a professional nurse. She can care for patients in the home, especially the chronically ill, the convalescent patient, or the physically handicapped. The approved training schools for practical nurses usually have a minimum age limit of eighteen years, but no maximum age limit is set for admission. The younger woman desiring to enter an approved school for practical nurse's training is usually expected to have at least two years of high school education. However, the eligibility of the more mature, older woman is not usually determined by age or educational background, but by physical fitness, personality qualities, general intelligence, and sincerity. A course in practical nursing usually takes twelve to eighteen months and concentrates on the care of patients who are not considered critically ill, but who suffer from a chronic ailment or a disabling condition; the convalescent patient; or the needs of the new mother and her baby. The practical nurse learns general household management, how to plan and cook normal nutritious meals, and how to prepare special diets that may be ordered by the attending physician.

Some hospitals employ nontrained women as nurse's aides who carry out less complicated and less responsible duties under the supervision of a graduate nurse. There is need for untrained women in every hospital, in the capacity of maids. They can add to the happy outlook of the patient by maintaining a cheerful atmosphere of cleanliness in his room or ward, by assisting in the serving of meals in an attractive and appetizing manner, and by many acts of kindness and thoughtfulness carried out in a cheerful and willing way.

Some women who feel they have not the qualities to withstand the emotional strain of constant contact with sick patients still have a general interest in their welfare. Such women have availed themselves of work in different fields associated with care of the sick. The dietician, for instance, who is responsible for the planning of meals, can stimulate the jaded appetite of many a patient. The laboratory technician, by skillful tests, helps a doctor in making a difficult diagnosis. The X-ray technician, the secretary, the record librarian, and many others work as a team in hospitals, clinics, and institutions. All know the sense of satisfaction that comes from work that in one way or another helps the unfortunate victims of illness and disease.

Many women miss an opportunity to enrich their own lives by not volunteering their services to the sick and handicapped in their community. This is especially true for the woman whose family has grown up and whose once busy life filled with the task of raising a family now seems dull and aimless. What great satisfaction it would be to her to know that she could make a contribution to society by devoting part of her time to the afflicted. Many jobs associated with the care of the sick, which can be handled by volunteer workers, are not always of a dramatic nature. Many are tedious and monotonous and may seem relatively unimportant, but no task is unimportant when it is a link in the chain which brings health and happiness to the needy. If a volunteer is sincere in her desire to be of some practical value in her community she must be dependable and willing to carry to a conclusion, even at personal sacrifice, any promise of responsibility she may have undertaken.

Many women do not realize that what appears to them an unimportant or ordinary talent can be utilized in the volunteer field. The woman who drives a car, for instance, can give invaluable help to a handicapped patient by driving him to a clinic for treatment. The good seamstress can help in a busy hospital by making garments or helping with the colossal job of mending. The woman who was a secretary before her marriage can brush up on her shorthand and typewriting and help out in the office of a hospital. The woman who has a hobby, whether it be painting, drawing, or playing chess, can always teach it to patients who are hospitalized over a long period. In times of epidemic and disaster, hospitals are eager for the help of volunteers. Some institutions caring for the aged or chronically ill use volunteer help as nurse's aides.

Women can be of service to the sick by volunteering assistance to raise funds for one of the many charitable organizations dedicated to restoring and maintaining the health of the community. Women can do much to correct poor environmental health conditions which exist in many communities, and they can prove real friends by helping with household chores or doing many tasks to bring comfort and gladness to ailing neighbors. Dr. Marcus D. Kogel, former New York City Commissioner of Hospitals, in making an appeal to women's organizations for nurse candidates and volunteer help, said, "I think the point of our argument to older women is that forty or fifty is not so old after all; that life really can begin at forty if one has the will to make it do so. I cannot, in truth, imagine people better qualified for practical nursing than mature and understanding women, many of whom have been schooled in the hard academy of family-rearing."

To any woman, aiding the sick will bring its own reward. To the woman looking for a career or profession which combines service, interest, personal satisfaction, and the opportunity for advancement and constant employment, nursing offers every assurance. For the woman over forty who is "looking for something to do," it offers opportunities to share her life's experiences with others. She can return to the community, for its welfare, that which she has taken from it, added to by her own individual pattern of living.

Nursing techniques are the means through which the kindness and love of woman can be brought to suffering humanity. The nurse must insist within herself, and in her association with patients, upon the genuine characteristics of her womanhood. The nurse is not to be prized and esteemed only for her professional proficiency. A real nurse has to be a real woman, true to her own nature. The modern tendency toward a cold, impersonal organization of human society must not be allowed to dominate the education of nurses. There can be no justification for trying to substitute exact efficiency for the wider implications of the nursing profession. It would be a mistake if increased standards of education were to bring about a completely intellectual approach on the part of the nurse toward her patient and replace the virtue of compassion so essential in the nurse. A nurse caring for the sick has to realize the sacredness of the human being. She must have faith enough to see God in a human soul no matter what the external conditions of the body may be. Her tenderness and sympathy must be a source of inspiration and encouragement and her love for God's human family must be shown in the mercy she extends even to "the least of these."

XII

HON. FRANCES P. BOLTON

Woman in Politics

JUST at the close of the Second World War three other members of the Committee on Foreign Affairs of the U.S. House
of Representatives and I were sent on a mission to Europe and
the Near East. We saw the tragedy of destruction in England
and France. The stench of death that was Berlin penetrated our
very souls. We walked through the rubble that was Warsaw
and its counterpart, Stalingrad. Everywhere we went there was
the hideous aftermath of war reflected with unforgettable
tragedy in the eyes of the women.

Returning from two weeks in Communist Russia with Moscow
as our center, we stopped in Rome to avail ourselves of the high
privilege of an audience granted us by the Holy Father. In his
gracious words of greeting he singled me out (the one woman
present), commending me for having recognized my responsibility as a woman to stretch out the walls of my home until they
encircled the world.

It is in such wise that I envisage woman in politics.

Politics has many connotations. Primarily it is the science and
art of government—yet it is also the machinery by which political
parties manage their affairs. Through this machinery the citi-

zenry expresses its will. Participation in these mechanics is both a privilege and a responsibility. We women of this free land have been recognized as full citizens: we have the franchise. We have become partners with men in this extraordinary enterprise which is the government of these United States. We, as women, bring to this partnership additional gifts, a different understanding, a new approach.

In recent years, when the scarcity of manpower pulled women into many fields heretofore not open to them, they proved their ability to do as well as, and in certain areas even better than, the men they were freeing for more dangerous assignments. So it would seem that women have proven a definite equality of capacity with men that cannot be disputed.

But let us not fall into the error of interpreting "equality" as "sameness"—an identical capacity! It is because the essential reality of our woman's being differs from the essential qualities of man that it becomes more and more important that our voice be heard and our counsel heeded.

Woman is the giver and the protector of life. She is the matrix of God's life on earth. It is around her that the family revolves, the unit upon which civilization is built. She is the mother, the teacher, the counselor, the focal point of love within that unit. In her hands rests the future, for her children are the future. Together with the man of her household, consciously and unconsciously, she points the way, she holds the light. We know so well that without the father, children are tragically insecure. It is he who faces the outside world and gives protection and strength. But it is the mother who is both inspiration and comforter within the family circle. It is from her that the children discover the joy of sacrificial service for the common good. It is from her that they learn that America is a nation whose trust is in God—whose strength lies in the belief that love is indeed the fulfilling of the law.

Women have influenced the destiny of nations down the ages.

In ancient India, in China, on the islands of the Pacific, there is historic evidence of their power and their vision. Egyptian history is filled with the names of queens who ruled alone or who shared equally with the Pharaoh the great responsibility of government. In ancient Greece and Rome, women played great roles of influence. We have but to turn to Europe to find Isabella in Spain, Elizabeth and Victoria in England, the Maid of Orléans St. Joan, who galvanized a nation into action only to be burned to death for her efforts. And in our own times as heads of states, we had Dowager Queen Wilhelmina of the Netherlands, and her capable daughter, the present Queen Juliana, with the second Elizabeth across the channel.

Out of the darkness that covers the earth today will come a new day. An era is being born which will recognize the basic need for woman's influence and judgment upon all levels. The world that is destroying itself was largely a world built upon the overemphasis on the judgment of men alone. It has had its rightful place in the evolution of man upon earth, but the complementary judgment of woman is now being added. The world that is tearing its way into new life will be a world where men and women share the responsibilities for its existence and work shoulder to shoulder, heart to heart, for its establishment and its growth.

We who live today have behind us the courageous women of yesterday who saw the vision and pressed ever onward and upward toward the light. We could not stand where we stand today had these women of other days not excelled in the great reform movements in every field of human activity. Who were some of them? There was Elizabeth Fry who pioneered in prison reform, Elizabeth Garrett who broke new ground in the field of medicine, Florence Nightingale who created an entirely new approach to the relief of human suffering which Clara Barton then instituted as the Red Cross in America. There was Octavia Hill who, by her tireless efforts, awakened society's conscience to the matter of decent housing. And there was Josephine Butler whose outcry that "Injustice is immoral, oppression is immoral, the sacrifice of the interests of the weaker to the stronger is immoral" could well serve as a guide-line in our own usages of political power. Closer to us, strong in her certainty of the right, we have our own Susan B. Anthony through whose zeal and indomitable will women were inspired to demand full citizenship. With her were such women as Carrie Chapman Catt, Jane Addams, Lillian D. Wald, and many others, whose lives contributed so much to the initial recognition of women as persons in a civil life.

Because they, and many who remain unsung, lived and worked and demonstrated women's capacities, the way was opened for women to take their place in all areas of national life. That they are doing so in ever increasing numbers is heartening indeed, for it would seem to show that there has come to women a definite recognition of the new part they must play if the world we are building is to be more nearly the world God meant it to be.

We have grown accustomed to speaking of the nation's manpower; it is a familiar term. But the newer term "womanpower" is still a little strange to us. We have been accustomed to thinking of ourselves as "the weaker sex." Indeed, we have thought of ourselves as a minority, lacking in power, rather than recognizing the reality of numbers and the consequent possibilities of influence. But the 1950 census brought to us the dramatic realization that we are no longer a minority, our numbers topping those of the male population by something like two million. This gives new meaning to the picture of women in politics. It means that we must assume the responsibility of numbers. It means that we must accept the fact that we have power, and use it humbly in true service to Almighty God.

Analyses of the 1952 election show that the women of this country, both rich and poor, rose up as a great tide and exercised their right of franchise as never before. As many women voted as men, and the various polls indicate that from 2 per cent to 4 per cent more women voted for President Eisenhower than did men. Important as this outpouring of women was, it is but a small part of what every American citizen who is a woman must do if government is to become the instrument of freedom envisaged by those mighty men through whom the Spirit moved when our Constitution and the Bill of Rights were inscribed.

We are agreed that the family is the unit upon which civilization is built. We are agreed that, theoretically at least, the man stands between his family and the outside world. We are agreed that within that family the woman is the spiritual and moral force which holds it together, from which its members draw the strength, the fortitude, and the knowledge with which to meet the problems of living, as they unfold step by step. I would enlarge upon the suggestion given me in Rome. I would say that in today's world life has taken on new aspects—the complex problems of an industrialized society have taken the mother from her weaving at the hearthside to the textile factories outside the home, to the offices, to the steel mills. The economic pressures of just bare living have forced women into industry all too often. Home has ceased to be a place of peace and close companionship. It has been invaded by a sense of insecurity, of danger and suspicion. It has all too often become a center of tension and anxiety where there is little chance for peace and love.

Just as women have moved out of the home into industry, children no longer learn the fundamentals of their education at their mother's knee. They have moved into mass public education in huge schools where today there is a shortage of more than 58,000 teachers and 300,000 classrooms. It is too soon to know what the outcome of such a situation will be—it is too soon to evaluate the results. Yet on every side we see the demoralization of the home, the deterioration of morals of both old and young. The family unit, the center of our civilization, is fast ceasing to have integrity. With their parents seldom at home can we blame the children if they no longer stay there? It should shock us wide awake to find that a recent report paints the tragic picture of one million children picked up by the police in one year—*young* children not even in their teens! Can we blame some of their mothers if they must be at work to make possible the food and clothing necessary to the life and growth of these very children? Such things as these are the necessities of life. They do not represent the luxuries for which, unfortunately, some mothers abandon their homes in an effort to accumulate more and more material conveniences and thereby deny their children the more important spiritual and physical comforts of motherly care.

What of the nurseries and the recreation centers to which these youngsters should be going? Why do so few exist? But equally important, we must be on our guard lest nurseries and recreation centers assume the parents' "rights" over their children. The right of authority over the children must always remain vested in the hands of the parents.

It is a God-given right as well as a civil right, and constitutes the very foundation of a free democracy. If this right of authority over children is ever transferred from homes where mothers are working out of necessity, to the organizations supporting the nurseries and centers, it would be a serious threat to our form of government and to the very institution of family life based on the law of God. The nurseries or recreational centers, whether supported by state or community organization, can help and assist the parents, or parent, in promoting the welfare of the child. They can offer care, recreation, guidance, counsel, and medical attention, but always with the full knowledge that the final decision in regard to such assistance for the child is solely up to the parents, (unless of course the parents are judged by court order to be incompetent). We have seen too much of the agony of parents in other countries whose children have been taken away from them and whose right to parental authority has been grossly negated to allow any infraction of this right ever to creep into any extension of our community nurseries and recreation centers.

For those children who need it, is it not the business of a woman to see that her own community finds ways to establish such extensions of the home as will protect them? Must she not go out from the confines of her home in order to secure such protection? The moment she steps across her own threshold bent upon such a mission she begins to assume her larger responsibility as a citizen. Fortunate indeed is the community whose women have accepted the challenge of today's world, for the moment one step is taken others follow in rapid succession.

This first step opens up a new world and brings to a woman an overwhelming sense of the need to know how these things are done and by whom. Almost automatically she asks where she may go to learn the methods by which she can make her opinions known. This usually leads her to a group of those who, like herself, have determined to do something about inadequate or intolerable situations. Before they are aware, they have become "women in politics." Once awakened, women rapidly develop an eagerness to understand, a determination to know, which can well change the course of living in their communities and so in the nation itself.

Awareness of her own community's problems brings recognition of the fact that they are tied into the problems of the county, the state, and of the nation as a whole. Politics become dramatically and vividly the climate in which she lives, for she realizes that we are all of us knit so closely together that this which she thought of as a thing apart is in reality the machinery, the structure, the method of daily living. She soon loses all sense of strangeness, for the matters which have carried her into this new aspect of life are all of vital moment to her as wife and mother.

Bit by bit she finds her way to the town council meetings.

Soon, perhaps, she is on the Library Board or the Board of Education. As another step to assuming actual responsibility she enlists the help of the various church groups, the civic clubs, the local League of Women Voters, the Veterans' Auxiliaries, the P.T.A., and she becomes one of a group of influential citizens. The walls of her home have started to move out into the community and she begins to realize that she is part of a nation and of a world.

Some there will be, and in increasing numbers, who will seek elective or appointive office. This is not an easy path. It requires, to be fruitful, peculiar gifts and special training and experience. Most of all, it requires understanding of and love for other human beings, a willingness to work and tireless energy. But the enormous number of women who will be recognizing their responsibilities as full citizens of a free nation will work quietly to further those matters which are most clearly theirs.

We cannot escape the fact that we have ceased to be a minority group. We have demonstrated the possibilities of our concentrated interest and determined action. No longer can we permit ourselves any apathy, any inertia. The welfare of the nation, even of the world, is in our hands.

Although we have not yet come to appreciate the full meaning of the fact that our financial holdings alone give us a basis for action in areas where such power can make our voices heard, we recognize a new attitude toward us in the market place. We hold title to at least 40 per cent of the nation's thirty million and more homes. We are the beneficiaries of 80 per cent of the life insurance policies of the country and 35 per cent of us carry our own life insurance. We are said to hold 65 per cent of the mutual savings funds of America and at least 42 per cent of all income tax returns are paid by women—as are 80 per cent of all inheritance taxes—and this means that there is in our hands economic strength we could well use. An even more potent force is ours in the area of retail buying. Fifty-five million of us are the retail shoppers! Would we not be taking a more realistic hold upon the influences that surround our children if we denied our economic support to unwholesome publications and stage and screen features? Concerted, intelligent determination must precede active political action if it is to be successful. The voice of woman can make itself felt. But if it is to be effective, it must be a constructive voice of reminder to all people that the family is the unit around which our civilization is built and that the structure of the family is as strong as its faith in God.

This is but a rough sketch of our backgrounds, of some of our potentialities. Let us look at our record in public service over the years for a moment, remembering that nothing so far-reaching as this sense of our woman's obligation to the nation bears fruit over night.

It was in 1786 that the first women (two postmasters) were accepted into federal service. In 1862, the U.S. Treasurer inaugurated the plan of using women in appreciable numbers to alleviate the wartime manpower shortage. In 1870, legislation was passed formally permitting the employment of women in the federal government service. Today it is estimated that approximately one fourth of the total roster of federal employees are women. Only about 1,000 of these occupy executive positions of marked authority in policy making and administrative fields. President Taft's appointment of Julia Lathrop as head of the then newly created U.S. Children's Bureau gave women their first appointment as chief of a major bureau. That post is held with distinction today by Dr. Martha M. Eliot.

Women are to be found in the greatest numbers in county offices. There is no county office that has not at some time been filled by a woman unless it be that of coroner. At least 12,000 women are serving today as county officials in 3,072 counties of the United States. They have taken the first steps across their home thresholds. On the state level, a recent check showed 304 women on the rosters of the legislatures as against 29 in 1920.

In the judicial field at least 125 women are on the federal and state courts, as well as on the domestic relations and juvenile courts where they work closely with local welfare groups and social agencies.

But it is not just on local and state levels that women are found. Congress has claimed 60 women since 1916 when Jeannette Rankin first took her seat in the House of Representatives. Today Margaret Chase Smith of Maine, with a background of nine years in the House, is the one woman in the Senate, while sixteen women are serving in the House. Women have held official positions in many of the departments and bureaus for a quarter of a century. In the State Department and the Foreign Service it was estimated that there are some 3,000 American women serving in 294 missions abroad, hundreds of them in the higher classifications, with 75 career women serving in Washington. Some 200 consuls and vice-consuls have been women—and several outstanding women, Mrs. Daisy Harriman, Mrs. Ruth Bryan Rohde, Mrs. Eugenie Anderson, and Mrs. Perle Mesta have represented us as ministers and ambassadors, while Clare Booth Luce was appointed our Ambassador to Italy and Miss Frances Willis, Ambassador to Switzerland is our first career ambassador.

With the establishment of the United Nations, an even wider field of influence opened before us. Here Eleanor Roosevelt has served with diligence. I, myself, was the first woman to be appointed a delegate from the Congress. It was not an easy trail to blaze—but she has shown an appreciation of the dramatic need of all nations for the contribution which women in particular can make to the great future that has opened the way to all who will follow.

All across the world, women are assuming greater responsibilities in the political life of their own people in order to build a world that will indeed be "closer to the heart's desire." Although there are still many lands where women do not have the franchise, yet in some of these they hold positions of far-reaching influence and great responsibility. Here in America, it is becoming more and more the accepted fact that we who are women have a contribution to make in the field of active politics. Women long active in political fields know that power lies not in the invasion of those areas of endeavor in which men excel, but rather in the areas where their very womanhood is a shield, a strength, a force. We know, too, that we are but the vanguard. We know that the full value of our contribution will not be made until all women throw open the windows and doors of their homes, not only to let in the sun and the wind of clearer perception and deeper understanding, but perhaps more importantly to let their own vision and humble determination to serve the Infinite Purpose of Life become a part of the active forces of national and international policy and action.

With the world in darkness and confusion, the increasing power of women in government, here and everywhere, is not a question of "equal rights." It is a question of the dramatic national and international need for the understanding women have of the fundamental life-giving truths. It is woman's primary function to give life, to renew life, to protect the young, to give them their first lessons in the art of living. It is our part to keep alive faith and hope and the certainty that because God is, we are.

It is no longer enough that we seek only to influence our men to wiser decisions, to better living. Those of us who are able to do so must seek office in every area of government. Those who cannot must find ways to encourage and strengthen those who can. Just as the individual must examine his own soul before he assumes duties which involve others, so must we who are women go deep into our hearts and minds to ascertain what it is that we have which is so vital to the full purposes of the Infinite. Once we are convinced and aware that only as we take upon ourselves these broad aspects of our womanhood can we hope to see the dawn of Peace, the day of Light, only then shall we give richer meaning to citizenship in this free land of ours.

Politics is the machinery of citizenship. Let us who are women take our places quietly, intelligently, and unselfishly within its organization, accepting in full measure the duties of such citizenship in a land established upon the immovable rock of trust in God. Politics needs an elevation out of its present context which tends to be exclusively temporal. It should take its true place in society in the service of human beings whose total lives are spiritually dedicated to God. Politics should be the development of true peace and prosperity of mankind; it is a link in the chain of total prosperity which is spiritual. Woman's duty is to reforge the link which binds politics to a higher order.

XIII

JANE M. HOEY

Woman in Social Work

THE contribution of woman to social work, as to other professions, depends upon: her nature and role in life—to reproduce, inspire, and conserve the human race; personal characteristics and attitudes essential for effective service; general education, training, and experience necessary for professional practice; enthusiasm for her work and a desire to improve continually its quality. Her contribution is conditional, likewise, upon a political, cultural, economic, and social setting in which women are free to participate in social welfare and other programs. Such a setting should include salaries and working conditions that will attract and hold qualified women and adequately compensate them to meet their financial obligations and enjoy a decent and healthful standard of living. What women social workers have done in the past may indicate what can be expected of them in the future.

Since the objective of social work is the promotion of human welfare, it is logical to expect that woman would make a substantial contribution to it. In their own family life and as wives and mothers, in spirit if not in fact, women are naturally concerned about the welfare and rights of other people. They have an opportunity for training and experience that helps them establish habits of mind and behavior that are a great asset in a social worker.

The emotions of women are deeply stirred by obvious human distress and they seek to relieve pain as soon as possible. But quick relief is not always feasible. Since women spend most of their lives in their homes, undertaking obligations they cannot shirk, they face difficult situations daily and learn how to handle them. They sensitize themselves to observing symptoms of pain or grief and not only give care but also try to determine the cause and do something to prevent recurrence.

Older female children in large families frequently are given, or assume, responsibility for care of younger children even at an early age. The assumption of this function in later life is not too difficult. Also, women accept discomfort without too much protest, endure the pangs of childbirth and the joys and grief of child care and other family responsibilities, and thus learn to face pain with courage and hope, and to help others do so.

Probably child care and training, likewise, have taught women to appreciate and communicate to others the fact that human rights have corresponding responsibilities and that personal growth, social adjustment, and satisfying and profitable relationships depend largely upon unselfish concern for others. The language they use may be different but the same idea is conveyed in a variety of ways. Women have learned to get real satisfaction from the act of giving, not so much to receive expressions of gratitude, but rather from the benefit the recipient of the gift derives from it.

Religious motivation has undoubtedly been an important factor in the decisions of many women to participate in social welfare programs and to train for the profession of social work. All religions stress respect for human dignity and rights, and the necessity of personal sacrifice and service in aid of the needy and distressed. Women, in larger numbers than men, if church attendance is an indication, seek the help of religion and are influenced by its precepts. They are sustained by faith that their efforts will be reinforced by spiritual aid. Thus a degree of humility enables woman to recognize her limitations and to seek help from all possible sources, divine and human.

All these feminine qualities and experiences are most helpful in conditioning women for social work and other professions. They make possible personal development and a manner of living that is satisfying and compensating.

Many of the basic principles of social work stem from our belief in the divine origin of man. Some of these major principles, which have a special appeal to women because of their personal philosophy of life, are: respect for the human dignity and personal rights of every individual; the duty of all men to promote these human rights in their personal and group relationships and through their government and private institutions; confidence in the potentialities for growth and self-direction of each person within his capacity; recognition of the family as the most important social institution for child care and training and for the progress of civilization; conviction that society has an obligation to make it possible for men and women to earn a living, to provide the essentials of life to those in need and to establish, through government and voluntary associations, rehabilitation insurance, assistance and service programs to prevent social breakdown and to promote the public welfare; assurance that men, given the opportunity to acquire knowledge and skills and use abilities, will raise their standards of living, spiritual and material, and will develop goals and ways of living that will be personally rewarding and socially desirable and productive.

Since these principles have been derived from religion and are also basic to democracy, woman agrees to them and works with enthusiasm for them. Social work presents one opportunity for their practical application.

Social work is a relatively new profession. Hence the outer limits of its scope and some of its functions have not as yet been clearly defined. However, knowledge and skills required for professional practice have been identified and are now taught in sixty graduate schools of social work in the United States and Canada. Frequently, women were responsible for or participated actively in the establishment of these schools. Using modern research methods, they have also been largely responsible for establishing its professional character.

Within the broad field of social work there are major functional classifications: case work—direct personal service to individuals and groups; group work—promoting the welfare and developing the capacities of individuals through a group process and strengthening interrelationships between groups; community planning and organization to raise standards of living and to secure support for specific services; social research; consultation; teaching; and administration. In 1950 in the United States, 75,000 persons were employed in social work positions; 50,000 of these were women. Seventy-six per cent were case workers or group workers or were supervisors of such activities.[1]

Training for social work is the same for men and women but employment opportunities and the nature and interest of the two sexes have influenced their selection of courses and their specialization. The majority of women select case work, psychiatric, medical, family and child welfare, and group work as their major interests. Men are more apt to concentrate on community organization and administration.

A large percentage of those employed in social work positions have had no training in a graduate school of social work. There is no legal regulation of social work practice but some employers require full professional training, and indications are that at some future time such training will be required. The difficult and complicated problems confronting social workers require the best possible professional preparation. This is true especially of psychiatric clinics, medical social work in hospitals, and voluntary family and child welfare agencies. A broad cultural background, with emphasis on the social sciences and the

[1] *Survey of Social Work Salaries and Working Conditions,* United States Bureau of Labor Statistics, 1950.

humanities, is considered the most desirable undergraduate preparation. Successful completion of two years of graduate study at an approved school of social work is required for a master's degree in social work and three or more years for a doctorate. Training consists of classroom teaching and field clinical instruction in a public or voluntary social agency.

The majority of students in schools of social work are women, although the numbers of men have increased substantially since the 1930's. During the depression, public welfare programs were greatly expanded and salaries of supervisors and administrators were raised. In spite of the fact that the number of students at schools of social work has steadily grown through the years, the demand for trained workers far exceeds the supply. More general recognition of the need for skill in providing social services, with rehabilitation and raising standards of living as objectives, accounts for this increase in requests for trained personnel.

The personality and attitude of the social worker are important in building sound social relationships. She represents hope to those seeking help. To know that she has no personal or agency profit motive in providing service, that she is in fact a friend who can be trusted, is a first step in building or reestablishing self-confidence. Little can be accomplished without this.

Willingness to listen is a great asset in giving assurance that any proposal for assistance will be based on a knowledge of the particular situation of the individual or group, and will take into account personal desires and objectives. In their own families, women have learned to be good listeners, to cooperate and to team play, and not to superimpose their opinions on others. By their questions and other indications of concern and understanding they can ease emotional strain and clarify issues and objectives.

But something more is required of the social worker than these general qualifications which should characterize any mature, well-adjusted person. The social worker must have special knowledge and skills if she is to help individuals, families, and groups to remove barriers that prevent their meeting their basic human needs, functioning to their full capacity, and contributing to community life. Knowledge of the economic and social forces that affect people are important, as well as information about community resources that are, or can be made, available to help people find a way to a solution of their problems.

Understanding of human behavior and motivations are also essential if, with the assistance given, the persons concerned move forward "on their own steam" as rapidly as possible. The independence and self-respect of recipients of social services must be strengthened, not weakened, by their contacts with a social agency.

The setting in which welfare programs operate affects the objectives, scope, and organization of social work and to some extent the technique utilized. The opportunity for women to participate in social welfare does not depend solely on their initiative. In the United States and in other countries striving to achieve a democratic way of life and a high standard of living for all people, social work programs have a common aim, are broad in scope, and have many different organizational patterns under public and voluntary auspices. Since individual, family, and group problems are complex and closely related to economic and social conditions, experimentation and demonstration of new methods of providing services or of solving social problems are encouraged. Professional and lay persons cooperate in performing appropriate functions in such projects.

In the totalitarian countries the role of woman in social welfare is quite different from what it is in the democracies. A small group of top government officials make decisions as to what social programs are to be undertaken and the methods to be used. Unfortunately, promoting the interests of the state and not the welfare of people is the objective of all activities. Labor shortages and pressure for production of material goods force most able-bodied women, as well as men, into the labor market. The maintenance of voluntary social agencies, especially those under sectarian auspices, is discouraged and resources to finance them are totally lacking or inadequate. Community organization to promote governmental or voluntary programs or to establish cooperatives, with objectives not in line with the predetermined plans of political leaders, would be out of the question. There are almost no volunteers with sufficient leisure to give time to the operation of social welfare programs, and professionally trained social workers would find operating in such a setting practically impossible.

Social work in the United States is organized and maintained under public and voluntary auspices, sectarian and nonsectarian. The consensus among social workers, as among the public, is that both public and voluntary social services are certainly desirable and should be adequately supported. Progress is achieved in the long run when freedom for all types of organized constructive effort is assured. Citizens by their vote and other methods of expressing their will to their legislative representatives can decide what social services they wish to support through their taxes. The number of people requiring services, and the cost, have largely determined the public programs. The special interest of the sponsors in providing service to a particular group and voluntary contributions determine the programs of private agencies.

Women, to their credit, in most communities have taken the initiative in arousing interest in the need for social services and have an important role in their management. Currently in the United States, women probably constitute the majority of board members of voluntary social agencies. Increasingly, also, women are being asked to serve on state and local boards of public welfare and other public agencies.

But the present situation in respect to the contribution of woman to social work cannot be properly evaluated without the perspective of her activities in the past. Thus it is necessary to

143

determine what occasioned the development of social agencies, what activities or programs were first initiated, what work was undertaken by women, what qualifications they had, and what skills they used in such activities.

Organized social work on a large scale can be traced chiefly to three major forces that have changed and are changing conditions throughout the world: industrialization and consequent urbanization, wars, and economic depressions and inflation. These situations have emphasized economic and social needs that are always present, to some extent, but go largely unnoticed by the public until periods of great strain when large numbers of people are affected.

In an agricultural economy, with a relatively youthful population, women extended many of the services performed for their own families to their neighbors and friends. Friendly visiting, counseling based upon personal experience and judgment, and direct assistance requiring little cash expenditure usually were sufficient to meet most recognized needs.

As urban, industrialized communities developed, requiring mobility in the labor force, few common bonds brought neighbors together for mutual aid. As populations grew older, more aged and disabled persons exhausted their resources and required financial aid and other welfare services. The number of children deprived of parental support and care because of death, illness, desertion, divorce, and illegitimacy also increased. Family ties were weakened or broken when parents stayed on the farms and their adult children gave up agricultural enterprise and moved to urban areas to engage in industry and commerce. The homes of married children in towns and cities were too small to house aged parents or dependent needy children of relatives. Likewise, incomes were often too limited to support two families when substantial cash outlay was involved. The complexities and impersonal nature of urban life further increased the problems and insecurities for individuals and families giving rise to a need for financial aid and related services. Finally it became apparent that some community facilities and programs were required to meet the needs of particular groups.

The same situation developed in respect to great need becoming obvious when war brought widespread destruction of property and loss of life or disability of large numbers of wage earners. This was true also in periods of economic depression, when industries shut down throwing many persons out of work and thus reducing purchasing power. These situations arose in the United States, England, and are arising today in many other countries that are in the process of industrialization, or are beset by wars and decreasing economic resources.

In many countries the same pattern of initial social organization was established. Largely as an outgrowth of church organizations and often manned by religious orders of women, institutions were founded by voluntary effort for the care of the sick, orphans, aged, and destitute. Since buildings are an ever present reminder of the generosity of givers, it was fairly easy to secure donations for this purpose. The needy, in periods between national catastrophes, were comparatively few in number and they could be hidden from public view behind institutional walls. This is not a reflection on institutions, but on their misuse.

When destitution and disability became widespread and could no longer be concealed from public view by placement in institutions, and cases of gross neglect and suffering came to light, then charitably inclined men and women decided something must be done to provide more adequate and appropriate care and treatment. Encouraged by the churches, they established relief organizations so that the needy would know where to apply and have assurance of some assistance. Some of these voluntary agencies were under church auspices, usually expansions of small, informal religious organizations; others were independent, nonsectarian agencies with their own boards of directors. In founding these more formal organizations with paid staff, the advantage of pooling resources and securing additional funds, through group effort, was recognized. These

145

increased resources were necessary in order to give emergency aid to the temporarily unemployed, and more adequate and continuing assistance to the increasing number of individuals incapable of self-support because of age, physical or mental handicap, or illness.

Usually, men supplied the funds for such agencies and women provided the services, either as paid workers or volunteers. This division of responsibility is understandable. As a rule, men earned the family income and decided what portion of their finances could, and would, be contributed for relief to needy people. Women, in those days, had little independent income. Those living in urban areas often had smaller families than those in rural areas. With fewer family obligations, some had leisure time to give to volunteer service.

For those women who wished, or were obliged to seek, paid work because of economic pressure, the care of children and the sick in institutions and the administration of relief offered good opportunities for employment. The salaries were not high but the character of the work gave emotional and other satisfactions. Almost any able-bodied woman could qualify for these jobs since the duties were not specifically defined and no specialized training was required, or even available.

England's industrialization came earlier than in the United States and its population had felt the impact of wars and subsequent economic recessions many times through the years. Therefore, some of its economic and social problems became conspicuous and received public attention before we became conscious of ours. It is interesting to note, however, that the same type of situation arising in these two nations at different periods brought forth the same response. Women, with qualities of leadership, became concerned about conditions and urged certain social reforms. English women, Elizabeth Fry, Florence Nightingale, Octavia Hill, demonstrated what could be done by informed, determined, persistent effort. Their success gave encouragement to a group of American women, Mary Richmond,

146

Dorothea Dix, Josephine Shaw Lowell, who functioned in a similar manner at a little later date.

From early days, in both countries, in the interest of protecting society, some public institutions were established and maintained out of tax funds in many communities. Legal action was necessary to assure confinement of certain groups, the insane, low-grade feeble-minded, adult criminals, and persons suffering from infectious diseases. The provision of institutional care for such persons was considered a public responsibility and little or no objection was raised to the use of tax funds for this purpose. Since the element of restraint was always present, and there was no segregation of groups within these institutions, employees were mostly men. Emphasis in selection of staff was on brawn and not brains.

As the population became more concentrated and living and working conditions changed, an increasing number of persons became dependent and disabled through industrial accidents, communicable and other diseases, and family disruption. Personal and family resources to meet the needs of such persons were inadequate or completely lacking and requests for aid far exceeded the resources of the voluntary agencies. Some sick and dependent people requiring long-time care, such as the aged and chronically ill and families with children but no wage earner, were added to the unsegregated, involuntarily confined, over-crowded populations of public jails or were placed in almhouses.

In the latter part of the nineteenth century and the early part of the twentieth, two different types of activity in social welfare by women leaders should be noted. Aware of the effect on human beings of degrading poverty, ill health, overcrowding, and unsanitary living and working conditions, they established settlement houses in slum areas in big cities. They lived in these settlements and organized recreational and cultural activities for their neighbors and helped them with their personal and family problems. Another trend in social work practice was the further interest and intensification of attention on improvement of

147

techniques and skills in case work and its extension to new settings, such as hospitals and clinics.

Notable among the settlement workers of this period were Jane Addams, who established Hull House in Chicago, Lillian Wald, the founder of Henry Street Settlement on the lower East Side of New York, and Mrs. Mary Simkhovitch who organized Greenwich House in the lower West Side of New York. Associated with Miss Addams at Hull House were Miss Julia Lathrop, Mrs. Florence Kelley, Miss Sophonisba Breckinridge and the Misses Edith and Grace Abbott, the latter coming somewhat later than the others. All these women had distinguished careers.

Miss Julia Lathrop was the first Chief of the Children's Bureau of the United States Department of Labor. This Bureau was established at the instigation of women, many of them from Hull House and other settlements. Its functions included research and promotion; its focus was on child health and welfare. Through the collection of facts and their interpretation by the staff of the Children's Bureau, Miss Lathrop contributed not only to the promotion of social and health programs but made a substantial contribution to the development of sound methods of research. Since social research in that period was only beginning, this function of the Children's Bureau helped to advance one of the newer areas of social work considerably.

Miss Lathrop had as her successors, as chiefs of the Children's Bureau, Grace Abbott, Katharine Lenroot, and currently, Dr. Martha Eliot. These women advanced immeasurably the health of women and children by the programs they initiated and directed.

In reviewing the contribution of women to social work in the first half of this century, the name of another woman social worker should be added to the honor roll. Frances Perkins, early in her career, became interested in immigrants and their adjustment in the United States. She served as secretary of an organization concerned with this problem. She was a friend and close associate of many of the settlement workers. She had founded and become the executive of the National Consumers League which through the years has been concerned with improvement of conditions of employment of women and children. Miss Perkins, and many other women, developed an intense interest in social reform when a large number of women lost their lives in a factory fire in New York City due to inadequate fire protection and overcrowding. Much desirable social legislation in New York State was enacted as a result of conditions highlighted by that factory fire. Frances Perkins got into the labor movement at that time and gave special attention to conditions of work of women and children. She was appointed by Governor Roosevelt as State Industrial Commissioner. As a result of the ability she demonstrated in that post, she was brought to Washington by President Roosevelt and appointed Secretary of the United States Department of Labor, the first woman in a Cabinet of the President of the United States.

In recent years, as more schools of social work were established, as social work content in service programs was more clearly defined and the knowledge and skills required for professional social work practice were identified and taught, the contributions of women in these developments have been distinguished. Many names should be noted but it is only possible, regretfully, to mention a few.

Gordon Hamilton, for many years a professor of case work at the New York School of Social Work, is so conspicuous as a leader in this field that her name must be included.

There are many women faculty members, deans, and assistant deans, who have made substantial contributions in the training of personnel for public and private social agencies. In addition, they have participated actively in community councils of social agencies concerned with extending and strengthening social services. Through the Association of Schools of Social Work, now a part of the Council on Social Work Education, they have raised the standards of professional social work education throughout the country. Notable in this group are Arlien Johnson, Elizabeth

Wisner, Anna King, Margaret Leal, Virginia Robinson, Jessie Taft, and Grace Coyle.

In the specialized fields of psychiatric and medical social work, group work, and community organization, the number of women who are doing effective work as practitioners and teachers are legion. It would be difficult for one not in those fields to evaluate and name the leaders. This, however, can be said: the women in these fields have not only perfected skills and adapted these to new settings but they have demonstrated what team play with members of other professions can mean in better quality of service to people. They have enriched the content of knowledge of practitioners and teachers of social work.

In community organization, women have shown and are showing what can be done in pricking the public conscience to provide essential social services as their predecessors did in the early days of social work. However, they work within organizations, collect basic data in a systematic manner, present these with their interpretation to individuals and groups that can take appropriate action. Thus their names do not appear as sponsors, but their satisfactions come from assisting others to do a good job and from seeing their efforts result in desirable social action. Only members of boards of directors, administrators and supervisors of agencies fully appreciate the work of such women. Everyone agrees, however, that trained social workers in these positions carry a heavy load of work and their contribution to social progress is considerable.

In 1950 when the Bureau of Labor Statistics of the United States Department of Labor made the *Survey of Social Work Salaries and Working Conditions* in the United States, it was found that about 60 per cent of the persons in social work positions had no professional training. This situation was brought about, largely, by the rapid expansion of public welfare programs in the depression when federal grants-in-aid to the states were made available under the Social Security Act. The trained social workers available were utilized in the Bureau of Public Assistance and the Children's Bureau to give leadership to the states in the establishment of new, or extension of old, programs of public assistance and child welfare. The state agencies used trained workers in key positions on the state staff and as supervisors in the big city agencies. In 1950, in the public assistance programs administering aid to the needy aged, blind, dependent children, and the permanently and totally disabled, there were 30,000 local workers (25,000 women) 83 per cent of whom had no professional training for social work. While these workers have shown ability in determining eligibility and seeing that financial aid is made available promptly to eligible persons, they are greatly handicapped by high case loads, low salaries ($2500 per year is the average), and inadequate supervision. Although efforts are made by most workers to provide welfare services aimed at rehabilitation and self-help, they have little time or training to do as effective a job as they would like.

When these public assistance programs were organized, it was clear that in-service training would have to be provided for the staffs of state and local agencies. The outstanding contribution to this field of social welfare education was made by Agnes Van Driel who devoted thirty-five years to professional education and agency training of social workers. One of her former colleagues, Olive Stone, now on the faculty of the School of Social Work at the University of California in Los Angeles, wrote of her: "As Mary Richmond distilled theory from practice in order to transmit agency-learned principles through the classroom; so Agnes Van Driel set into motion the other movement of the alternating current between agency and school."

Social work is daily growing in importance and presents innumerable opportunities for service to humanity through many different types of work in every county and city in the United States. Salaries for untrained workers are low—much too low for the responsibilities they are asked to assume. But trained workers, as has been pointed out, are in great demand and the salaries are consequently much higher. In recent years more women have been appointed to administrative posts. These are the highest paid positions in social work and compare favorably with top salaries in other professions and in business.

From the foregoing, it can be rightly assumed that social work is a field for women and that they have made a distinguished contribution to it. Their personal qualities and role in life make them excellent prospects if they will take the necessary professional training to qualify them for work in this field. One essential for successful practice must be emphasized. A deep conviction about the divine origin of human rights and faith in people and their potentialities for development, is indispensable to success in any phase of social work practice.

XIV

MARION TURNER SHEEHAN

Woman's Spiritual Role in Society

"WE are trustees of the future," said the young French widow, standing in the midst of her nation's chaos. "We cannot leave it to the next generation because they won't have seen what we have seen, and they won't understand." This quote from the foreword by Mrs. Anne O'Hare McCormick expresses her concern with the spiritual task of woman. She never ceased trying to alert women to this responsibility. Those of us who knew her well believe that this foreword, written just before her death in May 1954, is a kind of legacy. In it, she summons women in this country to a greater understanding of their spiritual role, to "be worthy of their spiritual heritage and deeply aware that they share the work of creation and mold the future." It is a summons to all of us who believe in God to join in a unified understanding of woman's spiritual role in society. Since the trusteeship of the spiritual future of this nation is largely in the hands of the American woman, she will want to "take a fresh look at herself" and contemplate the American scene in this age.

There is a vast difference between the philosophies of a

womanhood alive to God and of a womanhood existing without religious faith. Woman, as trustee of the spiritual treasures of the past and of the hopes for the future, can review her origin in God and draw from this knowledge encouragement and hope for herself and her children. She can recall to this generation the historical fact that every human person gained a unique value and elevation from the Christian ideal of human nature. This ideal impressed the spiritual value and the God-centered worth of every human being. These spiritual values made it possible for woman to achieve the place she now has in Western society. As this religious ideal was the force that exalted the status of every woman, it is the force that protects and preserves it.

THE ORIGIN IN GOD OF THE HUMAN RACE

There is usually an established order for operation, a hierarchy, in every organization if only for the sake of harmony. It is common belief that God's order for the human race is to be found in 1 Timothy 2:13, "For Adam was first formed, then Eve." A further reference to the Bible shows that under Divine Law man is designated to be the leader of society and woman his complement. There is no spiritual inequality between the two. The Book of Genesis shows the origin and unity of the human race. It declares that man and woman were to be one flesh, a unified principle in the generation of the race, meaning harmony and union of the body, the mind and the will. Woman received the right from God to be man's partner. In this Divine design, it is obvious that there is to be no conflict of the sexes; there is to be a unity of love and action since Adam loved Eve as a part of himself. Both are to work together for the benefit of humanity with the Divine Law as the basis for conduct.

If the Bible is rejected as a myth, woman will ignore her complementary role and strive to assume a masculine leadership in society. To those who believe in the Genesis account, such a role is contrary to the plan of God for the human race and is certain to cause disorder and unending battle between the sexes.

THE ROLES OF MAN AND WOMAN UNDER GOD

According to the design of the Creator, man and woman have a human nature composed of a spiritual soul and a material body. Their possessions of mind, will, and emotions are essentially the same. They both have the same destiny—eternity with God— which is the one true equality. They share an equal awareness of a dependence upon God, of an inherent dignity, and of an immortal destiny for their indestructible spirit. They can share a spiritual vision that gives eternal value to temporal labor. They can share a spiritual understanding that gives meaning to pain and suffering.

On this spiritual level, there was no difference between Adam and Eve. We know that each, as a spiritual person, was the image and likeness of God, but with physical and psychological differences ordered to meet the requirements of their different roles. Although woman's special duties to society do depend upon her individual endowments, yet her rights as a human being depend solely upon the fact that she is a person. Wherever man recognizes woman as his spiritual equal, his attitude toward her is respectful. Where God's standard of conduct is not recognized, man inclines to relegate woman to an inferior position. We do not have to delve into history to verify what happens to human beings when God's laws are ignored. Today, in occupied countries, men in power who are contemptuous of God's laws are treating both men and women as slaves. Receiving no respect for their spiritual dignity, these human beings are being subjected to hideous atrocities.

There may be careless resentment in some women at the difference in roles between man and woman because they have not stopped to comprehend its spiritual significance. But the difference does exist as in the beginning of Creation. The harmonious complementation of the two sexes preserves a balanced society and an enlightened civilization. Man, in his leadership of society, has a basic protectiveness and a supportive attitude toward life.

155

His special prerogatives are strength and aggressiveness. Woman has a sense of trusteeship of life in both the spiritual and physical meaning. The spiritual qualities in woman—her reserve, refinement, and compassion—complement man's characteristics by moderation. The source of these complementary qualities is in her spiritual life. For centuries, man has publicly acknowledged this spiritual influence of woman by his expressions in art, poetry, and literature. The symbol of womanhood is used in his portrayals of the virtues of justice, goodness, and sanctity.

A woman who would assume the masculine role in society violates her own nature and causes deep frustrations within herself. In married life, her husband would lose his rightful place as head of the home and her children would suffer under her too exclusive authority. Such a situation distorts the basic family structure as set up under Divine Law and dwarfs the personalities and abilities of its members that could have been developed more fully within a balanced family life. In a spiritually balanced family life, parents are complementary to one another with the husband having final authority vested in him by God. There are many families in America where women rule the roost and some impartial observers declare that American society is becoming matriarchal, that leadership in the American man has become sluggish.

In studying the gifts given to man and woman to fulfill their different roles, we know that although the human nature in both is essentially the same, it is not rigidly masculine and feminine in the individual. In number, feminine hormones and male hormones in both man and woman vary according to the individual and can be responsible for influencing personalities, yet they do not change the different roles of the basic sex involved, male or female. Also, in individual men and women, there can be noted wide differences in personality traits and abilities because of inherited natural gifts, educational opportunities, or environmental factors. There are men who are normally gentle and quiet, and artistic, and some women who are naturally forceful and boisterous, and inartistic. Yet each has a basic contribution to make to the other and to society as a man and as a woman, and there is no justification in drawing individual personality comparisons between the sexes in an attempt to discredit the difference in basic roles.

Many modern men and women, in pursuit of successful living, seem to study everything else except the difference in their own fundamental roles in society. Yet, in the case of woman, her feminine role becomes woefully inadequate unless she understands the total nature of man and his primary role in society.

Rudolph Allers, psychologist, says: "Women have an individualizing outlook, men a generalizing one." Although both man and woman have logical minds, they are logical in different ways. Man usually uses reason to plan methodically, calculate, and deduce; woman's knowledge is apt to be more spontaneous and her understanding influenced by heart and feelings. Because of her gift of the guardianship of life, she usually has an awareness of the human element in a situation. By nature, she is sympathetic, compassionate, intuitive; to be truly effective in her contribution to society, she combines intuition with reason. This intuition can be used not as the enemy, but as the ally of reason, and realistic thinking requires her combining both. The foundation of woman's quickness of decision in the face of an immediate problem is her intuitive grasp of the concrete and the vital elements of a situation. There are many events in the experience of life which cannot wait for studied decision but must be confronted suddenly and quickly. It is then, that woman's intuitive grasp of the concrete is especially valuable. The countless immediate decisions made by a mother is an example of this quickness of intuitive action.

Woman's natural subjective and emotional qualities generally modify her objectivity. But if she overemphasizes intellectual and objective thinking, she can weaken this modification which is most natural and becoming to her. If she works with excessive intellectual satisfaction, she deprives herself of originality and warmth, which are the fruits of her intuition and inspiring genius. A conscientious woman, gifted with a high degree of intellect, develops it by the design of God that everything created be used to its fullest capacity for the greater good. But it would be unwise for any woman to allow abilities of mind to triumph over her spiritual nature as a woman because woman makes her greatest contribution to the world as a woman, not as an intellectual. Woman's most unique and priceless possession is the gift of motherhood given to her by God. A gift not in the physical meaning alone, but in the spiritual as well.

THE SPIRITUAL MOTHERHOOD OF MARRIED AND SINGLE WOMEN

According to Divine Law, motherhood is not exclusively in the biological factor. The whole of every woman is adapted to motherhood, not only her body, but her soul as well. A woman mothers the human being in more than the physical sense. Such a motherhood of human beings requires qualities of mind and heart adapted to human relations on the basis of love and the whole person. Every woman, married and single, can give to her family and to society the maternal gifts of understanding, inspiration, sympathy, and encouragement. Woman's fundamental concern in motherhood is physiological, psychological, and social. Her natural altero-centrism modifies and tempers the drive of egocentrism; with its capacity for self-sacrifice it restrains self-indulgence. Her spiritual love can be a source of tenderness and a reservoir of strength. At critical times, it can rise to heroic action to contribute its genuine femine character to a faltering society. A superficial love is fragile and weak, sentimental and emotional, but a woman's mature spiritual love is man's most dependable ally in an hour of need.

A godless philosophy ignores the spiritual factors in woman's nature. It does not recognize that woman has the ability to emphasize love above sensuality; the living person above material achievement; the spiritual objectives of life above the earthly factors. The element of selfishness in modern philosophy can destroy woman's spiritual generosity by its emphasis on self-satisfaction on this earth, on the pursuit of self in pleasure, on material possessions, on inordinate ambition. On the other hand, spiritual motherhood, under inspiration of Divine Love, is outgoing and universal. In reviewing the *Gospel of Eve,* a satire on modern woman's self-interest, presented by Martha Graham in her repertory of theater pieces, columnist Walter Terry comments on the point of the piece:

> These gestures—the useless flutter of a hand, a shrug, a grimace of exasperation, a prissy manipulation of stage props—all contribute to a characterization of a woman whose whole life appears to be dedicated to self-embellishment, self-admiration, and the arrangement of surroundings to enhance that self.

The modern single woman in her wide area of association with people has the same qualities of nature to contribute as the married woman. And when the single woman consciously uses her spiritual gifts of motherhood, the meager definition of single life becomes obsolete. Everyone has to love and when the power of love in the single state is given a spiritual direction, it does not turn inward to self. In the single woman, self can become the idol of love if spiritual elevation is not present. Dr. Kimball Young, sociologist, speaks of this self-love when he warns, "Among the gravest temptations to the woman faced ever more obviously with spinsterhood is to regress to childish and early adolescent modes of action and attitude." With exclusive attention to her own personal interests, she becomes a little girl for herself to mother. To protect self, she immunizes herself to the risks of wider horizons beyond her daily pattern of idleness or of work, but immaturity is too high a price to pay for immunity.

When the single woman adjusts herself to a proper relationship with man in society, she learns the value of being a true woman and not a promiscuous lover. The oft repeated inquiry, "Are friendships ever purely Platonic?" receives a reply from Mr. Joseph Whitney, human relations authority:

Certainly. One of the surest signs of emotional maturity is the ability to form warm, lasting friendships with individuals of either sex, without any hidden or presumably sexual motives. Such friendships may be based on intellectual compatibility, similarity of interests, the sharing of ideas and aims, or merely on sympathetic temperaments. The man or woman who has never enjoyed such a friendship has missed much in his emotional and intellectual development.

The well-balanced woman will not want to confine herself to an ivory tower associating only with other women. She will want to extend her needed feminine qualities to men wherever it is possible and receive from men the enrichment to her own personality that their masculine attitude and companionship can provide.

The single woman can base her values in life not only on the body or the emotions, but on the spirit as well. She can keep the transcendence of the spirit over the body and not exchange this elevation for the sake of bodily or material values. She can realize that conjugal love is a part of love, not the total expression. In experimental psychology, sex is considered as a state, not as a lone instinct. It is a state made up of a number of instincts and many elements. The direct instincts are reproductive, paternal, and maternal. When sex enters into character, it endows the mind with the capacities accorded to sex, masculinity and femininity. Sex is for the conditioning of the whole individual with qualities and it is not entirely confined to actions and reactions directed toward physiological aspects.

A woman limits her understanding of the natural and supernatural order unless she sees that sex is for the enrichment and prolongation of life and that it is not all confined to reproduction. Since sex is a purpose implanted by the Creator of human life, it looks to the whole of life. There are many single men and women who give their lives to goals other than the reproduction of the species and they do so with the special qualities of man and woman created by God to enrich the race. There are many of these individuals recorded in history because of their accomplishments and contributions to society by way of spiritually dedicated lives. Society needs the prolongation of truth and goodness, of knowledge and love, as well as the bodies of people. These qualities are an important part of human life, the part that makes for the superiority of the human above the animal. It is this point that is forgotten by materialists, who look upon sex only for physical reproduction; that may be why the general attitude on sex today is at such a low level. The materialistic viewpoint is widespread and this philosophy is a concern to every religious-minded woman because it discards spiritual values. Its tolerance of moral laxity can weaken the spiritual fiber of our nation and soften us for attack by our godless enemies. Immorality and excessive living have ruined many a nation in the past. Dr. Pitirim A. Sorokin, exiled by the Communists in 1922, and since then a professor at Minnesota and Harvard, says:

Those families among us which frequently change husbands and wives, which fail in their duties to their children and adopt the moral code of the gutter are pushing all of us along the road to chaos. Greece, in the third and second centuries, B.C., "brought sex out into the open." We know, because there were Kinseys in those days, too—men who prided themselves on their objectivity as they calmly recorded the distressing picture of whole families getting together to indulge in promiscuous behavior. Adultery, prostitution, were so common that those who indulged were regarded merely as interesting fellows. But such a society was not able to summon the backbone to resist in the face of war or to endure the austerity program that might have salvaged their overblown economy. Soon the glory that was Greece was over and the mighty Acropolis was only a hillside strewn with ruined marble.

WOMAN AND THE MODERN CONFLICT

The philosophy of materialism arrives at a set of values in a so-called scientific way. It takes only the visible and tangible disclosures of the human being which are measurable. Such a set of values is based on the belief that man himself is the center of the world and God is not. These values are measured by their contribution to man as he is here on earth, without consideration of his life in God. This philosophy of life has its own codes of conduct, rules and regulations for daily living and working, with no recognition of God. Its effort is to achieve the fullest possible perfection on earth since a hereafter is denied. On the other hand, religion upholds the spiritual dignity of man and woman in earthly life with the promise of a perfect life in eternity. Its goal is union with God in the Divine Kingdom.

The materialist seems able to induce many religious-minded people to broad tolerance of his attitude. But he, himself, is loud in his protest that religion takes the extreme attitude and he remains firm in his intolerance of Christianity and belief in God. He discards the Christian philosophy of life as having no value whatsoever. Yet, Christianity recognizes material and earthly values, but in their proper order, placing the spiritual and eternal above the material. In Christian religion, both spiritual and earthly values are meant to combine in an orderly way to operate for the benefit of mankind. When woman surrenders to the idea of earthly values only, she gives up the dignity given to her by Christianity. She descends to an inferior role wherever earth-bound materialism prevails.

The attention given to material well-being and efficiency of operation has smothered many cultural and aesthetic values. As a result, woman's vision has often become circumscribed by material advantages. She has learned to accumulate these advantages as a matter of course with no elevation to spiritual thought. The higher values of knowledge, goodness, truth, and beauty have become more or less obscured by the narrow drive to accumulate material goods. This limited goal tends to keep the mind away from heaven and to focus it on the things of this earth. One of the serious challenges of our times is to keep a spiritual standard of conduct. Today's set of standards for human conduct, when separated from the spiritual, is filled with contradictions. If people try to live these contradictions, they can fall prey, perhaps unwittingly, to a pattern of hypocrisy and insincerity.

Secularism is another irreligious philosophy which believes in the total goodness of the human person, the unlimited progress of human society, the absolute right of the individual to judge what he thinks is for the good of man and humanity without regard for the rights and purposes of God. The principal tenet of its code is the acquisition of whatever brings pleasure here and now. Everything is judged not in terms of reference to a Divine Law that guides man, but in terms of the satisfaction that things give him. Secularism refers to some spiritual values but not for any religious reasons. We can recognize in this a modern reversal of the old saying, "Morals make the man," to "Man makes the morals."

When these philosophies establish codes of conduct based on the judgment of an individual alone, each one can take the direction which gives the most personal freedom, satisfaction, and pleasure. All conduct is then justified by calling it a "standard of living." Stalin, for instance, could have justified to himself all that he did from this point of view. With man making the rules, there is certain to be conflict among people in deciding what is of the most benefit. The obvious result is confusion of morals and codes of conduct with no hierarchy of values. Freedom, for example, when used without reference to standards established by God and nature, can become destructive. It can cause frustration in an individual as well as enrichment; it can degrade as well as exalt.

In the case of the women "emancipators" in this country, during the suffragette period, there are those who believe that many of these women magnified their freedom but minimized their sense of spiritual values. In trying to imitate the ways of man in society, they adopted mannish attire, brusque speech, and forceful action. Although we know woman has the right to compete with man in the business of the modern world, she has no right under the design of God, when doing so, to try to imitate man's

163

nature and discard her own. At her disposal in the competition of business are individual abilities of will, intellect, and specialization. But these are to be used not at the sacrifice of her feminine personality.

The fulfillment of a spiritual ideal and standard of conduct requires self-direction and self-mastery. It calls for the development of spiritual strength to keep first things first. The modern idea of letting things take their own course results in aimlessness and hopelessness. The theory of evolution, for instance, believes that a man automatically advances in his development on earth. This theory has taken a desperate course under existentialist philosophy. The existentialists believe man cannot direct his life, nor the currents and movements of life, toward an objective because he has no way of knowing what the objective might be. They believe he can only know the present and, as a pawn in world processes, he is a drifter on the stream of present experience with no rudder to direct his course. If this were the case, a human being would be no better than a kite in the wind. Instead of intelligently directing his life toward a dignified goal, he would blindly surrender to the day's experiences. In this way, man would not be the master that God intended humans to be in a temporal world; he would be at the mercy of natural events.

In modern psychiatry, woman may be taught a code of behavior which would not allow people or situations to affect her. Although this can provide emotional protection for a woman from outside influences, it can also deprive her of an opportunity to extend her womanly gifts to others. It could destroy in her the very nature and talent of womanhood to contribute itself in help to others. Psychiatry is helpful in analyzing personality, releasing tensions, and stabilizing emotions. It is to be highly regarded as a science, but in laying down laws for human life and conduct there are many who believe it is entering the field of moral philosophy for which it is not prepared.

Man and woman, under the Communist system, are judged on the basis of their intellectual and physical contributions to society without acknowledgment of spiritual values. The differences in their roles are minimized and they are considered collectively. From this collection of humanity, selection of the best from a productivity-to-the-state point of view is made by those in power. The cast-offs are flung into slave labor camps; the sickly ones are destroyed like weakened animals.

The humanistic philosophy of life concentrates on mankind as existing only on earth with no belief in eternity with God and acknowledges no difference in the roles of man and woman. An interview I had with a prominent woman book reviewer on a nationally known newspaper a few years ago was to obtain her point of view on woman's role in society. The following remarks, taken from my notes at the time, revealed her humanistic attitude:

I believe the most important consideration about humanity is its function to survive on earth. Work to maintain itself is the primary concern of each person. In this plan to survive, there should be no difference in the roles of man and woman. Each can be judged by individuality and by work performance. Woman is born to be a mother because she is organized to reproduce by a functional process. But she may not have, individually, the certain necessary aptitudes to rear children. She, therefore, can turn over the raising of her children to another woman with a developed vocational skill of caring for children. After World War I, I served on a suffragette committee investigating women's movements in various countries. When I visited Russia at that time and inquired about their woman's organization, I was told that in Russia there is no woman's movement but a *human* movement where everyone is considered on the same level and judged according to work abilities. Russia, even at that time, was far ahead of America in its attitude on equality for women.

There are some moderns who believe that in order to achieve a place, par excellence, on this earth, mothers can be separated from children whenever it is indicated that they have no "aptitude" for child-rearing. The idea of a "lack of aptitude" suggests an intellectual or psychological problem if viewed in the light of the spiritual concept of motherhood. With a deep spiritual relationship between mother and child, a profound love in the mother usually overcomes obstacles resulting from any personality problem unless there be a serious case of maladjustment, or extraordinary circumstances, which would justify her forsaking the natural duties of child-raising. This is the kind of spiritual love which extends itself to all members of a family unit and makes for the kind of peaceful home that gives spiritual strength to our nation.

WOMAN AND PEACE

In a world at peace, in a family of nations, there is need for the special endowments of the feminine nature—moral rather than physical strength, associative rather than competitive instinct, and patient observation with sympathetic understanding of national problems. In a world at war, peace and security depend on power, and there is special need of masculine strength, competitive instinct, hardness of purpose and abstract reasoning.

A faith in spiritual values, a practice of tolerance, these are the things that keep harmony between individuals. The basic virtues which guarantee the peace of a family are the same that guarantee peace in the whole human family, the family of nations. The refining influence of woman should not be confined to family living. Our civilization has provided her the opportunity to move into broader fields of action. In all fields, woman can exercise her unique influence for peaceful relations among people. She can help man root out prejudice, greed, self-complacency, which dig such deep chasms between people. She can help restore spiritual values to all fields of human endeavor. With her spiritual motherhood, she can view the world scene in the perspective of one family. That is why her delicate sensitivity to family values can warn of any social or political movement that threatens the home life of the nation and the world.

Since woman's realm is preeminently that of love, she holds the key to the world's division and hostility. Genuine love has always been the bond of union in the brotherhood of man. It is a force not sufficiently invoked and exercised in our times. The strongest support for alleviation of human suffering comes from woman because of the sacrifices she makes for human life. She can inspire society with the same sense of sacrifice for its members throughout the world. Her voice should be raised and her action intensified to promote thoughts and deeds of peace.

It can be said that woman never wins a war; she always loses whether she belongs to victor or vanquished. She can boldly ask if this heroism must be required of her endlessly. She has shown her willingness to contribute to the nation when the challenge of war has come. But she does not naturally resort to war but suffers it as a last fearful extreme. She must ask the leaders of the world if only political and economic issues are always to determine fatal decisions.

The world needs to feel woman's native abhorrence of violence and extremism. With no wish to *displace* man in the councils of the world, she should by her *participation* there contribute to the deliberations which affect the world. Only by the balance of her womanly sense of human values will the judgments of leaders be comprehensive. Her love of peace and her sense of human values will balance the political views of those who formulate the plans for human society. Woman, as trustee, must not stagnate in the dull acceptance of war and the war mentality. She must clear the way for the action and mentality of peace.

What the next generation will think to be important is what it is being taught now by the women of the world in their families. Woman's audience in her campaign for peace begins with her own family. This is the first place for her to reestablish spiritual thoughts and attitudes which will lead to world peace in the family of nations.